The Travel Guide for Her Elevation

CHANTORIA SCOTT

Text Copyright © 2021 Chantoria Scott

All rights reserved. No part of this book may be reproduced or used in any manner without the prior written permission of the copyright owner,
except for the use of brief quotations in a book review.

Scripture quotations taken from The Holy Bible, New International Version® NIV®
Copyright © 1973 1978 1984 2011 by Biblica, Inc. ™
Used by permission. All rights reserved worldwide.

To request permissions, contact the publisher at herelevation19@gmail.com

Paperback: 978-0-578-93234-7

First paperback edition: July 2021

Written by Chantoria Scott
Cover art by Jayden Williams
Layout by Jayden Williams
Photographs by Pexels

Printed in the USA.

Published by HER Elevation LLC.

Facebook @Her Elevation LLC
Instagram @her_elevation
Podcast Channel: Sublime Mindz

DEDICATION

This devotional journal is dedicated to women and girls that are in a place of growth, transition, healing, and finding themselves.

TABLE OF CONTENTS

1. You Are Her — 1
2. The Wait: Birthing Season — 7
3. Identity Crisis — 13
4. Social Media Poppin' — 19
5. Me, Myself, and I — 27
6. The Gift of Singleness — 33
7. Stay in Ya Lane — 39
8. Rejected, But Selected — 45
9. Always Forgive, Never Forget — 51
10. I'm Br(ok)en — 57
11. Fill Me Up, Lord — 63
12. Validate Me, Please! — 71
13. Girl, Wash Your Face — 79
14. No Boaz? That's Ruth's Man, Anyway — 87
15. Untie the Knot — 93
16. Mutual Disconnect — 101
17. Comfort Zone — 108

18. I Can do Anything Better Than You 113

19. GPS, Where to Next? 121

20. Level Up! You're Going Places 127

INTRODUCTION

Life is a journey, not a destination. You see, once you arrive at that place you've been hoping, dreaming, striving, and praying to get to, you'll soon find out that you now have somewhere else to go. As long as you have breath in your body, there is still work for you to do. What you thought was an arrival at your destination was actually only a pitstop for you to prepare yourself for your next level of elevation. What you perceived as your final destination was only a door that leads to a far greater journey. Life is what you make it. You don't get to choose what obstacles come your way, but what you can control is your response to your test and trials.

While you may have some people that envy you, some that disregard you, some that try to hold you back, and some that try to imitate you, your journey is your own. No one can duplicate you. When God formed you in your mother's womb, His plans for your life were already predicated. It's free-will that allows you to choose the route you'll take. Whether that be mountain top highs or valleys lows, whether it requires restarts, hiccups, stumbles, wins, loses, or breaks in-between, your journey is necessary, Queen. As I've been traveling on my own journey, I was instructed by God to set aside some time to reflect on my experiences along the way. Far too many times I asked myself the simple yet powerful question, Should I take this left? Or maybe I'll go right. I desperately needed somebody to help me out with this thing called life.

One day, I heard the Master's Voice. He called my name. He told me to pack my bags because some things were about to change. I've been set apart; I know I'm not the same. My destiny awaits, I had to stop playing games. I know I'm not alone; He's got me in His hands. I'll trust Him anyway, even when I don't understand His plans. The only thing I know is on this journey I'll go, and He'll be there when I need Him, until the very end. So, I leave with you this devotional journal as a travel guide for your journey of elevation. In this journal, I will be your tour guide, sharing my insight on the places I've been and the snares of the enemy that I've escaped, only through the power of Jesus Christ, The True Living God! God is the pilot on this journey. He is in control!

I'm only here to serve as a flight attendant. My job is to be of company to you, to inspire you, to empower you, and to influence you, as you travel on your journey of elevation. The most important thing to remember as we travel together is that God is leading us, as I'm guiding you, through these new levels of glory. Grab your travel guide and let's go!

-Your Tour Guide,
    Torre

DAY 1:
YOU ARE HER

Grace is without limitations and gifts are without repentance, so I encourage you to free your mind of all negative thoughts, feelings, and words spoken to you or about you that puts a limit on your ability to accomplish your goals and manifest your dreams. The only thing that comes to a sleeper is a dream, so WAKE UP! The only way you're going to catch that dream you're chasing is to consistently go and get it. Materials lost along the way can be replaced, but time wasted is gone forever. Having a vision with no work ethic is equivalent to daydreaming. You have to grind, you have to hustle, you have to be consistent to become who you're called to be, to do what you want to do, and to go where you're supposed to go.

Whether you desire to be an entrepreneur, a teacher, a writer, a performer, a doctor, or anything in between, your gifts will make room for you and bring you before great men. Never underestimate yourself. Everyone is unique and has been blessed with some sort of gift or talent. Your gift or talent may not be popular in society, but what you possess is necessary and important. Never minimize who you are by trying to be someone you are not. Embrace who you are, explore your uniqueness. The perfect God-given talents that rest upon your life are a blessing to you and others. No matter how hard your journey gets, you have the power to speak those things that are not as though they were. You have the power to stand up and say, "I will be who God has called me to be and I will rise up and break every generational barrier that held those back that came before me." I encourage you to push until your pain turns into strength and your dreams become reality. We are the chosen generation, we are a royal priesthood, a holy nation, and God's own special people (1Peter 2:9, NIV). Your past doesn't determine your future. What you once lacked doesn't determine your gain; who you are now doesn't determine who you can become. You're not too young, you're not too old, you're not too big, you're not too small, and you are not a product of your environment, but you are a result of surviving. You are fearfully and wonderfully made. Never give up on your dreams, goals, or visions. You were born a champion! You're the one that's going to change the game. You're the one that's going to finish strong. You are HER!

PRAY WITH ME

Father God, thank you for your unlimited grace and mercy. Thank you for making me who I am. I know you designed every detail of my life to work out for my good. Thank you for every mother, father, teacher, mentor, coach, and guardian you placed in my life. Whether they did a great job or a poor job in my life, I know, Father God, that you have always been there to fill the gap and connect every missing link in my life. I forgive every person that has attempted to belittle my dreams or stop my visions. I release every grudge I previously held against anyone who has wronged me in any way because I know that I must first forgive them so that you can forgive me for my sins.

Lord, give me the strength to keep pushing when I want to give up. Give me the confidence to step out on faith and pursue my dreams and visions. Help me to set my heart and mind on you so that I desire the things you have for me. Order my steps as I embark on new territory. Remove every distraction and every hindrance from my life. Surround me with people who are going to push me to be better and to do better. No weapon formed against me shall prosper and every tongue that spoke against my dreams, visions, and goals, I condemn. I reverse every negative word curse that has gone out against my name and I return it back to the sender. I break every generational curse off of my life and I divorce every covenant that is not of God that was passed down to me through my bloodline. I pray for peace in my home, joy in my life, and strength in every area that I am weak in. Lord, help me to see that I am who you say that I am, and I can do what you say I can do. Let my spirit be filled with you. And it is so, in the name of Jesus, Amen!

READ WITH ME

Jeremiah 1:5   Matthew 6:14-15   Isaiah 54:17

Matthew 15: 3-6   1 Peter 2:9

CONNECT WITH ME

1. What is your goal, vision, or dream?

2. What is special or unique about you and how can you use your gift/talent to glorify God?

3. What does God say about you in 1 Peter 2:9?

4. What's stopping you from making that dream happen, and what will you do next to make those dreams come true?

REFLECTION

DAY 2:
THE WAIT: BIRTHING SEASON

When you're in the process of waiting to be elevated, the wait can begin to feel like God is punishing you by keeping you in the same place. Your current position feels low, unsettling, uncomfortable, maybe even shameful. This place can be recognized as "the valley." You've been praying, pushing, fasting, walking right, talking right, even sowing seeds on fertile ground. You cut off all of your old boos and completely disconnected from all toxic relationships, but you feel stuck! You feel like you're still in the same position you were in before you started to do all of those things -- maybe even in a worse position. You've been doing everything right and you feel like you're ready to move up to the next level, so why isn't God moving on your behalf? Let's take a step back and evaluate this valley not physically, but spiritually.

First, I want to encourage you to change your mindset from "punishment" to "protection." Yes, I understand you've been working hard and you're looking to reap the benefits of your labor now. I mean we're only human and nobody wants to work hard now only to get paid later than expected, right? I want to reap the benefits of my hard work too, but through my own experiences of working hard and waiting for God, I've learned that patience is key. Sometimes, we want things too soon. A woman that's happily pregnant is excited and oftentimes will say things like, "I can't wait for my baby to arrive," or "I wish my little one would hurry up and get here." Although she is anxious about the birth of her unborn child, she understands the significance of going through the full process of being pregnant. A full-term pregnancy is defined as 37 to 40 weeks. If a woman gives birth to her baby any time before the 37 weeks mark, the baby is considered premature. Premature babies are at increased risk of death, infections, and serious long-term and short-term birth defects. The more premature the baby is, the more at risk they are for all of these complications due to being born before their due date.

Spiritually, you are pregnant with destiny, God's perfect plan for your life. Thinking of the complications and risks of birthing a baby prematurely will help you embrace patience and the process of waiting because you don't want to spiritually birth something too soon. Birthing your vision, your goal, your business, your career, or your marriage prematurely may cause you to go through complications. Waiting to give birth isn't always about you. When a woman finds out that she is pregnant, protecting the seed she is carrying becomes her first priority. Naturally, the mother will change her lifestyle, her eating habits, her environment, and even the conversations she takes part in because everything she does affects the seed that's growing inside of her.

As you carry your seed: your dreams, your goals, your visions, your calling, your gifts, and your talents, you have to shift your focus from your own desires to prioritizing what's best for the seed you're carrying. While you may be able to withstand the intense conditions of your current situation, the seed you're carrying is still in the process of developing an immune system to be able to fight off attacks such as word curses, manipulation, financial lack, disappointment, failed attempts, shots from the enemy, and counterfeit connections. While you're in your season of "carrying", don't despise the process of waiting. It is in your process of waiting that your seed will become equipped for the territory it's going to enter.

Waiting isn't always a direct reflection of deficiencies within yourself. Some pregnant women go past the 40-week mark, which means their baby is fully developed and equipped to enter the world, but the doctors tell the mother to continue to carry their baby until the baby is ready to come out. The territory that your seed is going to enter has to be ready for your seed's presence. Before a mother and her baby can be discharged from the hospital after giving birth, the mother must show the hospital staff the baby's car seat. Before a mother can bring her baby home, she has to change some things around in her home to accommodate the new addition. Before your gifts, talents, dreams, visions, and goals can be birthed into the world, some accommodations have to be made in the territory that your seed will dwell in. Waiting doesn't always feel good; waiting isn't always easy. Waiting isn't always comfortable. Waiting doesn't always make sense but trust the process! Your birthing season is coming!

READ WITH ME

1 Peter 2:2   Psalms 37:23-24   1 Samuel 15:22

Philippians 4:6-7   Isaiah 40:31

CONNECT WITH ME

1. What are you waiting on God to do for you?

2. Are you ready for the weight of the thing you're asking for?

3. Is your vision, goal, or dream ready for the harsh reality of the world?

4. What are the consequences of launching your vision, goal, or dream prematurely?

5. What does Philippians 4:6-7 tell you?

REFLECTION

DAY 3:
IDENTITY CRISIS

You're beginning to notice a change in yourself. You can't quite put your finger on it, but the people you used to connect with are no longer around. Daily phone conversations with friends that used to last for hours have now turned into minutes or missed calls. You find yourself driving past the places you used to go visit, and the type of guys that used to catch your attention can't even get the time of day from you now. Those friends that you thought had your back forever are now more distant than ever. All of your old, fleshly desires and habits suddenly don't bring you pleasure anymore. The things you used to brag about doing now make you cringe at the very thought of it.

To top it all off, you've been dealing with statements from family and friends like "you're acting brand new," "who do you think you are," "so you're too good for us now," or "she's bougie." Oh, and let's not forget about the statements "you switched up," or "I don't know who you are anymore." This is no coincidence or mistake; God is pulling on your spirit to have an identity change. The statement "you are what you eat" is often used in reference to a person's physical health, weight, and overall makeup of their body in comparison to what foods or drinks they are consuming. The reason you no longer have the craving for the people, places, and things of your past is that God has put you on a spiritual diet.

On this spiritual diet, you are going to drop off excess weight through detoxing. You will be cleansed of any harmful habits and connections lingering from your past sins. Dieting is always the hardest at the beginning of the process. I've often heard the statement "it's a mind thing" when speaking of dieting because once you've set your mind on the task at hand, you gain new strength to remain consistent in completing the process of change. Wherever the head goes, the body must follow. Anytime you start to take action towards becoming a better you, there will always be a level of resistance that attempts to hold you back.

Do this activity with me. Grab a small or medium-sized rubber band. Place one hand on each side of the rubber band and pull each side of the band in opposite directions of each other. You'll notice that it's only when you begin to stretch the rubber band beyond its original shape that you feel resistance. The farther you stretch the rubber band out of its original shape, the stronger the resistance becomes. This causes you to have to put more effort into stretching the rubber band. Now, let the rubber band go and watch it retract very close to its original form.

You'll notice how much easier it is for the rubber band to go back to its original form than it is for the rubber band to be stretched. This time, I want you to pull and stretch the rubber band until it pops. Popping the rubber band may cause some pain to your hands, but the pain won't kill you and it won't last forever. It is so much easier to retract to who you once were than it is to stretch into who you're called to be. Why? Because retraction brings a feeling of comfort but stretching requires perseverance and sometimes causes temporary pain.

One of the biggest resistance tactics the enemy will use against you is the presentation of memories of your old self. The enemy will manipulate you into thinking the life you had before you chose to walk in your new identity was better than the life you have now. When you give up your old identity for your new one, you're going to lose some things and some people are going to walk away from you. It's going to hurt for a moment, but remember, the pain is only temporary. When God removes things and people from your life, it's always for your good. After removing people or things from your life, God will bless you with something better or show you why the person or thing that was removed no longer fits in his perfect strategy for your life. Don't fall for the illusion the enemy presents to you. Many people are going to say you switched up, but the reality is you didn't switch up; you just tapped into levels that they can't comprehend. When you chose to walk in your new identity, it exposed you to levels that you've never experienced because your old identity was limiting your capacity.

Undergoing God's identity change is like having surgery. Before an operation takes place, the doctor requires their patient to be prepped for surgery. During preparation for surgery, all accessories must be removed from the patient. Jewelry, makeup, hair bows, lashes, acrylic nails, and anything else the patient has added to their natural selves for enhancement has to be removed before surgery. As you're being prepped for God's surgery, your accessories will be removed. Your old crew of friends that were up to no good, old partners, old habits, old desires, old routines, and everything that you added to yourself by choice has to be removed. Prepping for surgery doesn't always feel good. You may be feeling fearful of the end results, but God has not given us the spirit of fear but of power, and of love, and of a sound mind. It's time for you to be who God called you to be. You're not having an identity crisis... you're evolving.

PRAY WITH ME

Dear Heavenly Father, I come to you humbly as I know how to say thank you for choosing me. You could've chosen anyone in the world, but you decided that I was the person you wanted to use on the earth to do great works for your glory. I don't know how or when you are going to use me Lord, but I trust your perfect plan. I know there are habits, addictions, and toxic behaviors that I'm going to have to change, and I know there are people that I'm going to have to let go of. I pray for strength, peace, and guidance as I prepare to be made new by you. Lord, I ask that you guard my heart and mind as I experience new levels and new tribulations. Lord, help me make wise decisions and ordained connections as I undergo this identity change. Help me not to be blinded by the enemy's illusions, but to walk by faith and not by sight. On this day I choose you, Lord. In the name of Jesus, I pray, Amen.

READ WITH ME

2 Timothy 1:7	2 Corinthians 5:17
Romans 12:2	1 Timothy 4:12

CONNECT WITH ME

1. Has God been pulling on you to undergo an identity change? How do you know?

2. Do your old habits, routines, and behaviors no longer fulfill you? What do you desire now?

3. Who has a problem with you changing who you are now? They most likely have negative advice or comments to say about your new way of living.

4. What accessories have you added to yourself? What habits, friends, and foul behaviors have you added to your lifestyle to allow yourself to fit into certain environments?

5. What does Romans 12:2 say and how does it apply to your life?

REFLECTION

DAY 4:
SOCIAL MEDIA POPPIN'

Facebook, Instagram, Twitter, YouTube, Tik Tok, Snapchat, and so many other apps are currently dominating the social media world. I'm willing to bet my last dollar that you are using, or you know someone who is using at least one of these apps. I also enjoy using some of these apps for entertainment, business connections, news, and keeping in touch with friends and family. Social media has both positive and negative impacts on society. As the world of social media continues to grow and become more popular, I'm noticing a lot of people are using publicity stunts on social media as a coping mechanism to fill emotional deficiencies.

The attention people receive from displaying degrading behaviors online generates a temporary feeling of satisfaction or importance. For them, a short time of being in the spotlight has turned into a continuous craving for attention, nothing short of an addiction. So, is it safe to say that social media to some is what dope is to a fiend, what drugs are to an addict? The desire to go viral has influenced so many people to do dangerous, hurtful, and harmful things to themselves and others. Some people are willing to do anything for clout.

Pranks, fights, challenges, sexual acts, and even violent criminal activities are uploaded to social media daily in hopes of receiving a reaction from millions of viewers. People who use social media as a coping mechanism are usually struggling with depression, loneliness, brokenness, confusion, and emotional trauma. Bullies upload videos of themselves fighting in expectation of applause, attention, and validation from viewers who are sometimes associates in real life. Bullies that upload these types of videos are usually not who they appear to be. They seem to be big and tough on the outside, but on the inside, they are small and weak. They don't want to blow their cover, so bullies continue to use their physical advantages to create a 'tough girl' image for viewers. The winner of the fight in the video feels on top until the hype dies down and the viewers are talking about another post or situation that doesn't pertain to them. This leaves the bully right back where they started: depressed, lonely, broken, and willing to do anything for clout. So, the cycle continues, as the bully pulls another publicity stunt in hopes of gaining attention for another short-lived moment of satisfaction. Never to receive real joy, only temporary clout.

    Social media bullies aren't limited to the people that upload videos of themselves fighting; some social media bullies post unauthorized photos or videos of others so viewers can chime in on their posts. They criticize and make fun of other people's posts and photos. This usually causes the person who created the original post to feel embarrassed and humiliated over a post or picture they originally thought was cute or worth sharing. Social media bullies thrive off the attention they receive at the expense of other people's pain. They openly gossip about sensitive situations others are going through. They expose information they've been trusted with to keep a secret. Social media bullies love to keep a negative spotlight on others in hopes of no one ever airing out their dirty laundry. No matter how hard they try to justify their actions by claiming to be joking or just having fun, there is never an excuse good enough to make cyberbullying cool or respected.

    A quick word of wisdom: the same way you can't take back words after they've been said, a post on social media has the potential to be forever. Yes, there is a delete option, but there is also something called a screenshot. Think before you speak and consider the consequences before you post.

As bad as social media bullies are, in my opinion, the most disguised publicity stunt being used as a coping mechanism on social media is #RelationshipGoals and #LifestyleGoals. Ladies, girls, teens, and young women, please don't believe all of the hype and don't fall for the illusions. Now, I'm not saying everyone posting about their relationships and lifestyles are frauds. My point is you're only seeing one side of the story and you better believe it's only the side they chose to share that's being posted. Use yourself for an example. When you take a picture to post on social media, there is a process you go through before you complete the post. There are angles, cropping, editing, filters, lighting, and captions that all need to be perfect, in your opinion, before you post the final result online. We all do it. Social media gives each user the ability to control the narrative about themselves being presented to the world.

This leaves room for counterfeit information, half-told stories, and hidden truths. People don't show you their process because no one likes to publicize their weak moments, their flaws, or insecurities. There is nothing wrong with admiring a person's success or being inspired by their post, but don't be deceived by what they choose to show you.

There is always more to the story. The whole story doesn't always have to be associated with negativity. It may be a wealthy person posting their luxurious car, but what you don't see are the countless hours of work, time, and investments they had to make to get to the place they are now. Maybe there's a post about a woman, her husband, and their child living happily ever after, but what you didn't see is that the woman actually went through heartbreak, abandonment, and abuse before she met the man of her dreams. She had several miscarriages before she was blessed with her beautiful miracle baby.

So, be careful what you ask for and don't be envious of others' accomplishments. Be inspired, be encouraged, and be motivated by positive posts on social media while also setting your own goals and moving at your own pace to achieve them. Your story is still being fulfilled. It's okay if you don't have the car yet; it's okay if you don't have the husband and family yet; it's okay that you haven't arrived yet. It is not your responsibility to live up to social media's standards, but instead, you must hold yourself accountable for using social media networks responsibly.

Using social media responsibly means having self-respect, self-control, and self-love when posting photos, videos, and statuses of yourself and others. Never use likes, shares, or double taps as a method of validation. Social media isn't always a reality. While some viewers may choose to keep scrolling past your posts, remember you're popping in real life, baby girl. Using social media responsibly also means you only communicate with well-known sources and people. Don't allow the gift of gab from wolves in sheep's clothing to suck you into a dangerous situation. I don't care how cute they are, how sweet they talk, or how innocent the situation seems to be. NEVER plan to meet up with ANYBODY you just met online. This includes meeting up in public places.

You are a precious jewel. Many will admire you and many will want to have you for different reasons, but you must protect yourself from thieves looking to steal your life, your peace of mind, your body, and your soul. Last but not least, using social media responsibly means holding yourself accountable for your actions. We've discussed different types of social media bullies. Review your actions and adjust accordingly. Technology is advancing rapidly and so are social media and other networking/communication apps and platforms. There is nothing wrong with using apps and being a part of the social media world as long as you're responsible during your usage.

PRAY WITH ME

Dear Heavenly Father, I come to you with thanksgiving for the knowledge and wisdom that I've gained today. I thank you for your protection, your grace, and your mercy. Lord, I pray for those that have embarrassed me, spoke ill of me, wronged me, and hurt me. Vengeance is yours, Lord, and I pray that you will turn the hearts of every bully on social media and in real life so that they are healed and filled with your love. I pray that they no longer desire to bring others pain.

Heal me, Lord, of any hurt or pain that I carry from bullies and wolves in sheep's clothing. I forgive those that have hurt me so that I too can be forgiven of my sins. Forgive me, Lord, for my wrongdoings, known and unknown. Forgive me for the times I caused others pain as a result of a reaction I endured from my own pain. Continue to protect me and watch over me daily. Help me to become more aware of my actions and the actions of those around me. Give me the spirit of discernment so I don't fall for the gift of gab. Help me to understand the intentions of people who desire to connect to me.

I shall never look to social media for validation because I know you created me with purpose and value. I am who you say that I am, and I can do what you say I can do. Lord, help me to be free of lust in every area including the lust of my eyes. Show me how to work for my goals and visions while being on one accord with your will for my life. Give me patience, Lord, to wait for your perfect timing in my career, in my relationships, in my education, and in my heart's desires. Help me to fall in love with my purpose and not the lifestyle of others. Thank you, God, for hearing me. In Jesus' name, I pray, Amen.

READ WITH ME

1 John 2:9   Ephesians 4:29   Leviticus 19:18

Romans 12:18-19   1 Peter 5:8

CONNECT WITH ME

1. What actions do you consider to be social media bullying?

2. Whose lifestyle and relationship have you been admiring on social media and why? Do you know the whole story?

3. What can you do to keep yourself safe while using social media?

4. Are you being a social butterfly or a social media bully? How can you change this if necessary?

REFLECTION

DAY 5:
ME, MYSELF, AND I

You're off of work, you're out of school, you have no plans, and all of your friends are busy. You've eaten all of your snacks, you're caught up on all of the latest episodes of your favorite T.V. shows, and now you're BORED. Your actions while being bored will reveal your true colors mentally, physically, spiritually, and emotionally. If you need the presence of others to have peace of mind, then you have forfeited the power you possess over your own peace. You've given your power over to people you *think* you need in your life to be happy, to have fun, to feel important, or to feel loved. Because you have forfeited your power over your peace of mind to those people, their absence now has the ability to manipulate and control your mind.

You will encounter many temptations during times of being alone because the enemy knows when everything around you is silent, he has the opportunity to speak up. If you begin to listen to the words of the devil, you will begin to do things that are out of your character; things that you know are wrong. You'll find yourself in places you know you shouldn't be and connecting with people that are toxic and have negative intentions for your life. Being bored can be compared to being idle. I once heard my grandmother say, "idle hands are the devil's workshop."

Anytime you are sitting idle, you give the devil room to manipulate your mind. You should always have things at hand to work on in your spare time. Your goals are a great place to turn your focus to when you're bored. If you aren't writing out long-term and short-term goals for yourself, now is a great time to start doing so. You should never run out of goals. Once you've accomplished one goal, set a new one in its place. Having goals creates a continuous need to work on the goal itself or work on whatever it is that's hindering you from achieving that goal. There is always something you could be working on that will benefit your future. A woman that doesn't work, doesn't eat! So, a woman that sits idle and doesn't prepare herself for the things that she has been asking God for, will not receive them because she is not equipped to handle the weight of the things she's requesting. God doesn't waste blessings. But He will put them on hold until you show yourself approved to be able to handle the weight of what you're asking for. This principle applies to you.

    Think of a person that lifts weights. When they first start lifting weights, their trainer doesn't allow them to pick up the heaviest piece of equipment in the room. The trainer gives the trainee a lighter piece of equipment to help build strength and confidence. Just because the trainee told the trainer they want to be able to lift 300lbs doesn't mean the trainer is going to allow the trainee to attempt to do so. The trainer knows the trainee isn't ready to lift that amount of weight yet, so they continuously work with the trainee to get them to a place of being able to handle the weight of what they are asking for.

    Peace of mind doesn't always come freely; it's something you constantly have to guard in order to keep. When you're busy working on your goals, studying God's word, and guarding your peace of mind, you don't have time to look anywhere except straight ahead, all while focusing on the things God has called you to do. When you're idle, sitting around, and doing nothing, is when you have time to look behind you at the negative things you used to do. That's when you spend time searching to the left and to the right for someone's attention that persuades you to participate in an unhealthy lifestyle. You become distracted and fearful of your future that's unfolding as you continue to attempt to accomplish your goals. The enemy will place things like depression, suicidal thoughts, lust, confusion, regret, insecurities, and temptation at your door when you allow yourself to sit in boredom. The enemy wants to rob you of your peace of mind. Usually, when there is something important behind a door, there will be a guard placed in front of that door to keep what's inside safe from an unauthorized person attempting to enter the door. Productivity and proactivity are the guards standing at the door that leads to your peace of mind. Not having anything positive to do when you become bored is like telling your guards "productivity" and "proactivity" to take a break. When guards abandon their posts, it leaves the things that they were guarding in a vulnerable position. Anything unguarded is open for attack or invasion by the enemy. The enemy will walk right in and disrupt your peace of mind. Keep your guards up, set goals, get active, and stay productive. Your peace of mind is too important to lose.

PRAY WITH ME

Dear Heavenly Father, thank you for enlightening me today. Through the good times and the bad times, Lord, I know you never left my side. When I feel like I have nobody to talk to, when I feel nobody cares about me, or when I'm lonely, Jesus I know you're the greatest friend I could ever have. Lord, forgive me for not being a good friend to you. I've ignored you and chose other people's presence over yours, but I now understand the importance of guarding my peace of mind so that I can remain focused on the goals, visions, and dreams you have placed inside of me. Now, I will use my time of idleness to hang out with you and work on things that will benefit my future. Give me the strength to disconnect from people that are distractions in my life. Give me new ideas, new visions, and new goals to focus on. Help me to chase after you like never before. Let the desires of my heart be that of your will for my life. You're an amazing God and I thank you for listening to me. In Jesus' name, I pray, Amen

READ WITH ME

Jeremiah 29:11-13   Proverbs 16:27-29

CONNECT WITH ME

1. What do you do when you're bored?

2. What are your long-term and short-term goals? If you don't have any, create some now.

3. What are you waiting on God to give you? Can you handle the weight of what you're asking for?

4. Why is it important to guard your peace of mind?

REFLECTION

DAY 6:
THE GIFT OF SINGLENESS

There are always multiple sides to a story that involves more than one person. The most significant part of the story isn't the part that you've already heard; it's the part that you haven't been exposed to that holds the most weight. If you're always seeing and hearing stories about relationships and marriages, it creates a biased perspective on being in a relationship and being married. I'm not saying that the stories that you're hearing and seeing are false. I'm simply saying that it is possible the narratives you've been hearing have persuaded your overall view towards a certain belief because you've only been exposed to certain parts of the story.

These one-sided stories I'm talking about are displayed everywhere on social media. Social media is famous for its #RelationshipGoals or #MarriageGoals accolades. By no means am I hating or being envious. I love to witness love, but sometimes we get caught up in the fantasy of social media and put unrealistic expectations on ourselves and others. I guarantee you, the reality behind some of those posts isn't the side of the story that's being shared. Social media has its way of highlighting single women as sad, lonely, or desperate, but rarely do you see highlights of the single women that are happy, satisfied, and genuinely enjoying their singleness. Social media isn't the only platform handing out one-sided narratives on singleness.

Have you ever been to a singles conference or women's program and you were expecting to learn about the journey of being single, but the topic of discussion was something along the lines of waiting for marriage? The speaker was probably a married woman that is seasoned in the area of marriage and ministry. You heard all about the process of waiting and preparing to be a wife during your season of singleness. You learned the proper way to date and be involved in relationships. You heard about the perks of marriage, the challenges of marriage, how to survive marriage, and you even heard about how much of a gift it is to be married. Am I saying this information was incorrect? Absolutely not! It is definitely necessary to hear these things for future references if marriage is something you desire, but in my opinion, there should be more conversations about the gift of singleness. I believe that single women are coached on how to be a girlfriend or wife so much that they begin to long for and desire relationships and marriage with such an intense passion that they miss out on experiencing their singleness as a gift. It is not a curse to be single no matter what age you are. I don't know who created the 20's time clock, but I can attest to being one of many women who has heard you're supposed to be well in your career, have a house, husband, and starting a family by the time your mid 20's roll around.

    Some women feel the need to be in a relationship because they think being connected to someone proves their worth to others. Being in a relationship doesn't validate your level of beauty or your value as a woman. So many single women are forcing themselves into toxic relationships and marriages because they've been persuaded by a society that believes owning the title "taken" is more important than actually being happy and at peace. A marriage or relationship ordained by God is a beautiful union that should be celebrated and discussed. Singleness ordained by God is a beautiful status that should be celebrated and discussed with the same enthusiastic spirit as relationships and marriage.

    I honestly believe that when single women are celebrated more often in their singleness instead of encouraged with fantasies about what their life will be like when their husband arrives, more single women will be more accepting and open to their own lifestyles. I personally desire to be a wife, so the purpose of this devotion is not to discourage marriage, but to uplift women in their relational desires, whether they're single and waiting on a husband or single and uninterested in marriage. It's okay to desire marriage. It's okay to desire to remain single. No one status is better than the other. The important thing to remember is, to be honest with yourself about your heart's desire. I recommend you take some time to read 1 Corinthians, the entire seventh chapter. There you will find several benefits of singleness in comparison to marriage. Understanding the gift of singleness will help single women function at their full and best potential in all areas of life, including kingdom work. Whatever your preference is, understand that singleness is just as honorable as marriage. Whatever season you're in, enjoy it, embrace it, value it. A title doesn't validate your worth.

PRAY WITH ME

Dear Heavenly Father, thank you for loving me unconditionally. Thank you for staying by my side even when I tried to leave yours. Forgive me, Lord, for rejecting and despising my gift of singleness. Enlighten me, Lord, of the beauty and responsibility that singleness provides. Help me to unlearn false narratives about singleness and redirect me to a new way of thinking. Teach me how to strengthen our relationship because no relationship is more important than the one I have with you, Lord. Teach me how to enjoy my season of singleness. Prepare me for my heart's desires, whether it's to become a wife or to continue my life journey as a single woman. I need your wisdom and guidance to mold me into the person you've called me to be. Close my ears to confusion and shut my eyes to worldly distractions. Create in me a clean heart and a renewed spirit. Give me the strength to stand up for what I believe and the courage to operate in the manner that you've conditioned me. Disconnect me from anyone or anything that is persuading me to go against your will for my life. Grant me peace, love, joy, and patience in this season of my life. In Jesus' Name, I Pray, Amen.

READ WITH ME

1 Corinthians 7 (Entire Chapter)

CONNECT WITH ME

1. What is your current relationship status? Are you truly happy? Why or Why not?

2. Why is singleness a gift?

3. What are some things that you could do to strengthen your relationship with God?

4. What are your heart's desires in regard to relationships? What could you do to better prepare yourself to receive what you're asking God for?

REFLECTION

DAY 7:
STAY IN YA LANE

    I left home later than usual, so I was in a bit of a rush to get to work on time. Traveling in the right lane on a two-lane road, I came to a red light. In my lane, there were two cars ahead of me. The left lane had no cars in it and there was an opportunity for me to switch from the right lane to the left lane. I would be the first car in line instead of the third at the red light. As I was about to shift over to the left lane, I heard the Holy Spirit say, "Stay in your lane, this is prophetic," so I listened and stayed in my lane.

    When the stoplight turned red, a car rolled up to the light in the left lane and took the position of first place. Let's call this car "Purple". I remained in my position as the third car in line in the right lane. While the light remained red, the car that was in first place in my lane made a right turn, causing a shift forward for the car in front of me. The shift forward caused my position of third place to become second place. The light turned green and being that Purple held the first-place position, that car moved further along down the road than I did. Suddenly, the car in front of me made a right turn causing me to shift from second place to first. I continued to drive at my normal speed, but I soon became close in distance to Purple. I became so close that my front bumper was in alignment with Purple's back bumper.

    Unexpectedly, Purple swerved into my lane and then back into the left one, causing me to press my brakes to avoid crashing. I didn't get mad or blow my horn; I just kept driving as I had been all along. Then, all of a sudden, Purple had to slow down because traffic began to build up in the left lane. As I approached the next light, I needed to shift from the right lane to the left lane; the right lane became a turning lane and I needed to travel straight ahead to reach my destination. As I checked my mirrors in preparation to switch lanes, I saw Purple, which was once in the first place, lagging behind. This gave me enough room to shift over in front of Purple in the left lane. I remained in the first-place position for the rest of my journey to work. I arrived to work safely and on time.

When I reached my destination, the Holy Spirit spoke to me and said, "Stay in your lane."

In your lane, it looked like you were behind and when you looked over to the left lane, you saw what seemed to be a quicker and better position because you would've moved from third place to first place instantly. It seemed like the car that rolled up in first place while you sat in third place had a better position. It appeared that the first-place position would allow them to arrive at their destination quicker than you. Your obedience to staying in your lane when I told you to do so allowed me to shift you forward from third place to second place in line.

After this shift took place, it still seemed as though you didn't speed up. When you move how I say move and when I say to move, you will find yourself gaining more ground towards your destination than if you would've done things your way. The car swerved in your lane causing you to have to put on brakes. As a result of this, it caused your car to slow down, making you feel like you weren't going to make it to your destination on time. This was only an attack of the enemy in an attempt to make you crash and delay your arrival time. When you stay in your lane, the lane I created for you, there's no devil in hell that can stop anything that I set up. In this season of your life, your obedience is necessary for you to win. From the beginning, when you were in third place and saw what seemed to be a quicker lane, I had already gone ahead of you and knew that the left lane would turn into traffic later on down the road. Every lane that seems to be a quicker route to your destination isn't always the best journey to go on. Not only did I elevate you from third place to first place in your lane when it was necessary for you to shift to the left lane, but I also allowed you to shift to first place in front of the car that previously held that position. I cleared the path for you. I made room for you to operate in your rightful position when it was your time to do so. You could've shifted to the left lane in the beginning, but it wasn't your time then. If you try to move before I give you instructions to do so, you'll get caught up in traffic. The left lane was your lane from the beginning, but it wasn't time for you to take your position in that lane until later on in the journey.

Although you've seen your new lane, don't shift into the position until I say it's time. There are no quick routes to the destination I made for you. The enemy is only trying to manipulate you into shifting too soon. There are no shortcuts on this journey and some things that look like delays are really protection. When you stay in your lane, I will elevate you from last place to first place. I will make you the head and not the tail and I will do it in front of those that thought they had stolen your position. What they didn't know is that when it becomes your time to take the position that I said is yours, I will clear the lane and make room for you. And you will make it to your destination on time.

READ WITH ME

Proverbs 1:7   Matthew 20:16   Psalm 27:14

Philippians 4:6-7   Romans 8:28

PRAY WITH ME

Dear Heavenly Father, I come to you as humbly as I know how, saying thank you for your love, your peace, your joy, your direction, your correction, your protection, and your guidance. Thank you for being who you are, the Lord of Lords and King of Kings. Forgive me, Lord, for being anxious on my journey. Forgive me for stepping out of my lane and doing things my way instead of trusting the plan you have for me. Teach me how to wait on you. Teach me how to move when you say move and how you say to move. Show me the way to your heart. Help me to understand that illusions are sent to distract me. Give me the strength to stay the course even when it looks like I'm never going to get to the place you promised me. Give me ears that hear your voice above the noise of defeat. Give me wisdom in every area needed on my life's journey. Continue to mold me as I let patience have her perfect way. I trust you. In Jesus' name, I pray, Amen.

CONNECT WITH ME

1. Where are you going? What's your destination/your purpose in life?

2. Are you trying to take shortcuts because you don't like to wait?

3. What is God saying about the journey you're on?

4. What are the benefits of doing things the way God says to do it and when He tells you to do it?

5. What does Philippians 4:6-7 tell you?

REFLECTION

DAY 8:
REJECTED, BUT SELECTED

But the Lord said to Samuel, *"Do not consider his appearance or his height, for I have rejected him. The Lord does not look at the things people look at. People look at the outward appearance, but the Lord looks at the heart"* (1 Samuel 16:7 NIV)

Israel chose a king for themselves named Saul. God rejected Saul because Saul was disobedient to His instructions. So, the Lord sent the Prophet Samuel out to go anoint the next king of Israel. The Lord told Samuel exactly where to find the next king but did not tell Samuel the name of the boy to anoint as king. Samuel carried a horn filled with holy oil that would only pour out when placed above the head of the new king God had chosen.

When Samuel arrived at the place where The Lord told him the king would be, he asked the father of the residence to call forth all of his sons because the Lord had chosen one of them to be king over Israel. The father of the residence, Jesse, had eight sons, but he only called forth seven of them. Jesse did not think much of his eighth son, David. He was the youngest and least favorite of the father's children, so Jesse didn't bother to call David to the important event.

When Samuel saw the seven sons Jesse called forth, there was one that really caught Samuel's eye. This son looked like a king, talked like a king, and walked like a king. Samuel began to say, "Surely the Lord's anointed stands here before the Lord" (1 Samuel 16:6 NIV). But the Lord replied to Samuel, "Do not consider his appearance or his height, for I have rejected him, The LORD does not look at the things people look at. People look at the outward appearance, but the LORD looks at the heart" (1 Samuel 16:7 NIV). So, Jesse began to call all of his sons up one by one to see if the oil would pour from the horn on top of their head —signifying they were God's chosen king. After Samuel tested all seven of the sons and the oil still remained in the horn, he began to question the father.

    Samuel told Jesse that none of the seven sons he called forth were God's chosen one. Samuel then asked Jesse if he had any other sons. Jesse admitted that he had one more son that was left to work in the field. Samuel demanded that Jesse call forth his last son. When the eighth son David came forth, the Lord said, "Rise and anoint him; this is the one" (1Samuel 16:12 NIV). So, Samuel placed the horn above David's head and the oil began to flow from the horn down his head, signifying he was anointed as king. David was anointed king in front of his father and brothers and the spirit of the Lord came upon David from that day forward.

    Are you like David? Are you ignored, mistreated, unvalued, unnoticed, unloved, underestimated, and misunderstood by your family? Do your peers at school or coworkers attempt to exclude you from events, celebrations, and activities because they say you don't fit in their circle? They talk about the way you dress, the way you speak, how your hair looks, the color of your skin, the type of car you drive, and they even talk about the place you call home. Sometimes, the people around you can make all of your unique qualities seem like a curse instead of a blessing. When people can't comprehend your level of uniqueness, they tend to reject you rather than accept you.

    Being set apart isn't always easy or fun, but never let someone else's opinion of you cause you to become shameful of your uniqueness. If you're not careful, you'll find yourself mourning over what God has rejected. If you're too busy focusing on who has rejected you, you'll miss the fact that it was actually God rejecting them from being a part of your life because they're not ordained to tag along on your journey of elevation. God is such a good God that on this journey of elevation you're on, He'll provide you with everything you need to reach your destination. He will reject any person or anything that is not beneficial to your destiny. The pureness of your heart may cause you to be rejected by boys, girls, parents, siblings, friends, and loved ones, but it is your selection by God that will cause you to rise above all negativity. Embrace the unique qualities that make you different from others. Don't be afraid to humbly be who God has called you to be in front of those that call you a nobody. One day, when God sees fit, he will raise you up and proclaim that he has selected you to do great works in front of those that have rejected you.

PRAY WITH ME

Father God, thank you for creating me. Thank you for my physical features, my personality, my differences, my gifts, and my talents. Most of all, thank you for giving me a pure heart. Lord, grant me the wisdom to understand who you created me to be. Give me the confidence to walk boldly in your image, being set apart from worldly idols. Lord, let not my heart be hardened towards those that have rejected me, neglected me, disrespected me, and bullied me, but allow forgiveness to flow continuously through me. Protect me from all hurt, harm, and danger as I continue to seek your face daily. May I always see my uniqueness as a blessing and not a curse. Lord, give me the strength to keep pushing, to keep trying, and to keep trusting you on this journey of elevation. No longer will I mourn over what has been rejected in my life because I know that one "yes" from God overrides every "no" anyone has ever given me. You're a good father and I love you. In Jesus' name, I pray, Amen.

READ WITH ME

1 Samuel 16:7	Isaiah 49:15
Matthew 5:8	John 15:18

CONNECT WITH ME

1. Who has rejected you and in what way?

2. After reading this devotional, how do you feel about being different from others?

3. What does Isaiah 49:15 say about rejection from a parent?

4. How will you keep your heart pure in times of being misunderstood and mishandled?

REFLECTION

DAY 9:
ALWAYS FORGIVE, NEVER FORGET

It's over! No, I mean it, it's really over this time! The relationship has officially ended. You've made it through that week of ridiculous back-to-back phone calls, novel text messages with beginning, middle, and end paragraphs, and a thesis statement on why he, all of a sudden, loves you so much and needs you in his life. In your proceeding to ignore all of these things being said, you begin to receive death threats, suicidal threats, crying voicemails, oh and let's not forget the mind-blowing insults because you won't fall for any of those attempts to make you take him back. Or maybe, it has been a week of you constantly checking your phone to see if he finally replied to any of the messages you've sent pouring your heart out to him.

Maybe you've been on social media monitoring his profile and the profile of the girl you think he's interested in. You just can't understand how life has been so easy for him since the breakup. Either way, you begin the process of mentally and emotionally beating yourself up about being in a relationship with that person. "What was I thinking," "Why did I put up with his mess for so long," I know I could've found someone way better than him," "How could I be so stupid," and "I hate myself for this," are some of the things you say to yourself as you reflect on the relationship. The feelings of guilt, hurt, shame, and defeat pile on you like a ton of bricks.

Cry! Let it out! I want you to experience this temporary moment of pain because I want you to acknowledge the feelings this relationship has left you with. When you're finished crying, dry every tear and know that better days are coming. Never forget those tears; they will keep you from ever having to cry them for the same reason again. Now, it's time for forgiveness to take place, not for their sake, but for yours. The first person you have to forgive is yourself. Forgive yourself for falling for *potential*. When you put expectations on potential, it leaves room for disappointment. There were many times you thought about the potential your ex had to be a good guy if only he would stop drinking. If only he would stop smoking, if only he would stop hanging out all night, if only he knew how to control his anger, if only he would go to church with you, then things would change, and he would become the good guy that you knew he could be.

    You have such a big heart that you always try to see the best in people, but reality is, everyone isn't going to operate at their best possible version of themselves in life. Potential exposes the ability to develop into something or someone greater in the future. Potential is not a definite destination. It is a glimpse of destiny guaranteed to be reached only if one completes the developmental process required to master skills in order to turn them into permanent character traits.

    Just because a man has the ability to fix cars doesn't mean he's going to operate as a mechanic. He will only use his ability to fix cars to operate as a mechanic if he chooses to maximize his potential. If he never becomes a mechanic, it's not because he doesn't have the skills to fix cars, it's because he chose not to operate at his greatest potential. While you were looking at his potential to become a mechanic, he never even looked at himself as a man that can fix cars. You saw the gifts and the talents, but he never even intended to use his skills for greater works.

    Now, it's time to forgive the person that has caused you all of this pain. Forgive them for using their potential to manipulate you into thinking they were striving to reach their destiny when really, they were only distracting you and pulling you further away from your own success. Forgive them for attempting to minimize your worth in hopes of you never maximizing your potential. Now that you have forgiven him and yourself, total healing can take place. May this be a lesson that you never have to learn again. Never forget, but always forgive.

PRAY WITH ME

Father God, in the name of Jesus, I come to you with a heavy heart. I've given my heart away to the wrong people and the pain is unbearable. I always thought if I did well that good would come right back to me. It was through this process that I realized not all people have good intentions, so I can't expect good from those that are set out to use and abuse me. Lord, it was you that gave me this heart, so I pray that you show me how to use the love that flows from it correctly. Teach me, Lord, how to love from a distance and how to guard my heart and make wise decisions so that I'm no longer fooled by counterfeit romances. I forgive those that have hurt me so that I too may ask for your forgiveness today. Mend my broken heart, Lord, and give me the strength to move forward. Fill me with your unfailing love as I continue on this journey. In Jesus' name, I pray, Amen.

READ WITH ME

Colossians 3:13   Proverbs 4:23
Psalm 34:18   Proverbs 3:5-6

CONNECT WITH ME

1. What events happened that led to this breakup?

2. Overall, was there more pain or happiness in the relationship?

3. Why is it important for you to forgive but never forget?

4. What does Proverbs 3:5-6 tell you?

5. What will you do differently in your next relationship?

REFLECTION

DAY 10:
I'M BR(OK)EN

    Great! Another day you have to prepare yourself to face family, friends, co-workers, classmates, and society. You feel like you've been hit by a truck, to say the least. You can hardly breathe, and your eyes are swollen and red from continuously crying. You don't want to do anything except curl up in your bed and let your heart bleed out the pain. You've become quite the master of disguise though. So, you leap up out of your misery and put your game face on. You've created a perfect fake smile that shines bright like a diamond. You know how to give such a magnificent, bubbly laugh that you forget there was no real joke being told.

    Girl, you deserve an Oscar for that performance! You're so good at pretending everything is okay that you almost believe the lie yourself. That is until your show is over, and your day comes to an end. Now you're left to face the reality of the real you, the broken you. You've been weighed down by a combination of toxic relationships, bad habits, heartbreaks, bitterness, unforgiveness, unfaithfulness, soul ties, and generational curses for so long that you've taught yourself how to live two lives. A life of pretending to be happy and the life of the reality of your brokenness. No matter how good you are at pretending to be someone or something you're truly not, there will always come a time of exposure.

    The Lord did not intend for you to have to pretend to be happy. He wants you to have joy, love, peace, happiness, and so much more. The only way you'll be able to experience these things is to give God total access to you. I know you think you're a tough girl, but God has a way of breaking down even the toughest of hearts. Sometimes, God will allow you to reach your lowest point in life before he steps in to save you. Sounds a little cruel, but in all actuality, God loves you so much that he will allow you to try things your way to show you that you can't do it without Him. When you finally realize you can't do it alone, you can call on God to help you and he will step right in and get you back on track, according to his will and his way for your life. God allows you to be broken so that you'll reach a point of total surrender to his will and his way for your life. When you are in your weakest moments, God is at his strongest in your life. In your weakness, take your hands off the wheel and let God have complete control.

The moment you tell yourself the truth: that you're not okay, that you need help, that your heart is broken, that you're hurting, confused, and don't know what to do, is the very moment that you start the process of healing. To identify these things about yourself and admit that you need and want help is a major step to take, and I'm proud of you. But, in order to receive complete healing, you must give God access to every dark space in your life.

Think of a shipping warehouse, for example. When the large transfer truck arrives at the warehouse, the driver backs the truck into a port until the door of the trailer connects to the door of the warehouse. The truck is there to either receive items from the warehouse or to drop items off at the warehouse; therefore, there is an exchange scheduled to take place between the truck and the warehouse. The truck is in the correct position, but the exchange still cannot go forth until the warehouse opens its door and gives the truck access to what's inside. Once the door of the warehouse is open and access has been granted to the truck, the process of unloading and loading can begin. God is like a truck. He is in position, waiting for you to give him access to what you have hidden inside of your heart. He has bought some things to exchange with you for the things you already have.

God has brought joy, unspeakable joy, to exchange for your sorrow. God has brought a peace that surpasses all understanding to exchange for your troubled heart and mind. God has brought the love that can cover a magnitude of sins through his Son, Jesus Christ, to exchange for every sin you're holding on to. God has brought forgiveness to exchange for the bitterness and grudges you have toward those that have wronged you. God has brought healing through the stripes on the back of his son, Jesus Christ, to exchange for your sickness, disease, or health condition. God has brought wholeness to exchange for every broken place that's buried within your heart and soul. God has brought protection to exchange for any hurt, harm, or danger sent your way. There's nothing that you need that God hasn't brought in His truck to give you. You are like the warehouse.

From the outside, you look well put together, but on the inside, there is so much going on that no one knows about because you've kept it hidden for so long. You've prayed and asked God to help you and he has arrived with His truck parked outside of your warehouse with everything you need inside. God is a God of free will, so the only way he can unload the things he has brought to you and load up the things you've been storing inside is if you open up the door and let him in. Give God access to all of you. Open up every door to every hidden place so that an exchange can take place. Praying and crying out to God is a good start, but it isn't until you give God total access to your situation that you can receive everything he has for you. God is at your door. What are you going to do?

PRAY WITH ME

Father God, in the mighty name of Jesus, I come to you saying thank you. Thank you for answering my call. God, I called on you to help me and you showed up, but I never gave you full access to what I've been holding inside. Since I called on you, you've been here patiently waiting on me to allow you to come in. Forgive me, God, for getting upset with you because my circumstances and conditions have not changed. I now understand that it wasn't you that didn't answer my call, but it was me that never answered your knock at that door. On this day, God, I give you access to every hidden place. I give you access to my life, access to my family, access to my grades, and my job. I give you access to every relationship and friendship I'm involved in. I open myself up to be cleansed by you. Rebuild me, God, from the inside out. God, I want to exchange everything I've been holding on to for everything you've been waiting to give me. You are free to do whatever it is that you need to do in me, through me, and for me. God, I thank you in advance for complete healing and freedom. In Jesus' name, I pray, Amen!

READ WITH ME

Psalm 55:22   John 10:9   John 14:6

CONNECT WITH ME

1. Are you ok, or have you only been pretending to be?

2. Who or what has hurt you and caused you to have to pretend to be ok?

3. What is keeping you from giving God total access to the pain you have hidden inside?

4. What does Jesus say in John 10:9?

REFLECTION

DAY 11:
FILL ME UP, LORD

If you have a glass of tea filled midway, is your glass half empty or half full? Whether you say half empty or half full, technically both answers are correct. Your answer to this question is somewhat a reflection of what you think about yourself and how you feel about your life. I know you're probably asking, "what does that question have to do with my life", but flow with me for a moment while I explain. If you said the glass is half full, that indicates you most likely have a positive outlook on life. No matter how bad the situation that you're in is, you always find something to be thankful for or happy about. It shows your level of faith and determination.

Materialistically, you may not have as much as you desire, but you take what you have and make the best of the situation. Now, if you said the glass is half empty, that indicates your desire to have more. You're most likely unsatisfied with your current situation and it's causing you to feel drained, lonely, and unappreciated. You want better for yourself, but it just seems so much easier to stay down at the bottom than to try and rise up to the top. You're halfway to your breaking point and fear, doubt, depression, suicide, pain, and addiction are knocking at your door. A half-empty mindset is a cry for help because you feel like you're getting ready to lose your mind.

Here's the good news: regardless of if you feel like your glass is half empty or half full, there is a savior named Jesus Christ that will never leave you or forsake you. Your glass is never actually half empty or half full when you add Christ to the situation. It's just an illusion that you're missing something. Physically speaking, the other half of your glass is filled with air, but spiritually, the other half of your glass is filled by Jehovah El Shaddai, my Lord God, my supplier. God Almighty is a supplier of all needs and a filler of every void.

Sometimes your birth mother or father may only provide you with half of what you need to feel complete or whole. Maybe your mother is loving and caring, but she doesn't provide you with the knowledge and wisdom needed to survive in the world without her. Maybe your dad is financially present, but he's always physically absent, so he constantly misses important events and never shows you affection. Maybe your mom is a walking time bomb, very loud, aggressive, and demanding. She's never soothing or approachable for advice or compassion. Maybe your father mastered the art of inconsistency. Poor communication skills, many missed milestones, continuously canceled plans, and countless broken promises are his specialty. Or maybe he's a "sometimes" dad. Sometimes he shows up, sometimes he keeps in touch, sometimes he provides financially, sometimes he's kind and affectionate, but sometimes he's not.

  I could go on and on describing different types of mothers and fathers, but only you can confirm your own parental situation. What I am about to say may not sit well with you and I'm not making an excuse for any of their behaviors, but sometimes your parents went through some of the same things in their young adult life that you are going through now. And because they never experienced or learned a better way of living or parenting, they continued to display the same toxic behaviors they were taught. A person can only act, say, or do things according to their level of understanding. In other words, when you know better, you do better.

  So, what if your mother and father never knew how to give you a better life than the one you received from them? What if they were working with a half-empty glass and they poured everything they had into you, but it was only half of what you needed? Your parents may have left you with voids to fill, but God has always been there to make sure your glass wasn't left empty. We can't physically see God, but he has always been there. We often make the mistake of trying to use other people to fill the other half of our glasses with the time, attention, love, and affection that we felt like we needed but never got. The thing about using other people to fill voids, instead of God, is the people will never be able to fill you up because they only have an ounce of what you really need. For a while, it seems as if you're happy and complete, but soon you notice that you're still unsatisfied. This is because the person you chose to fill your void doesn't have the capacity to maintain what you possess. So, they go from being a temporary filler to being an unwanted strain. They begin to take from your glass instead of filling it...leaving you worse off than before you allowed them in your life.

  Let's say you get caught up hanging with a group of girls who are mean, liars, troublemakers, and bullies. You attach to them because they give you the attention or time that your mother didn't give you. Maybe you have become emotionally and sexually confused because there is another female giving you the attention, affection, and compassion that your mother or father didn't offer. So, it makes you feel attracted to the same gender as yourself, but really what you're attracted to is the feeling of having voids temporarily filled. Or maybe you desire the relationship of a male figure in your life so deeply that you often engage in toxic relationships with different guys. They're not good guys; they just know your weakness because you have confided in them about your past and they use it against you by giving you the one thing your heart desires but draining you of everything else you already had.

  When you stop blaming your parents for how your life is going now, then you will stop looking for someone to give you what your parents did not give. When you start turning to God to fill the voids of your past, then you will stop viewing your glass as half empty and see it as half full. Unfortunately, you don't have control over what happened to you as a child, but what you do have control over is your healing. You are responsible for your healing so that you may live in freedom in both your present and future. Every breath you take is of the present and every breath coming next is of the future. You don't have to wait long to be healed. Healing is literally available in your next breath. Just breathe and allow God to be everything your heart ever desired. Your glass will always be full no matter how much you think you need to fill the empty space. God is already there, so your glass is already full.

PRAY WITH ME

Dear God, thank you for communicating with me. Thank you for always being there for me. Even when I couldn't feel you, I know you never left my side. I have been through many painful days in my life that only you and I know about. Time and time again, I made the mistake of turning to people, thinking they would ease my pain, thinking they would love me how I wanted to be loved and thinking they would give me the desires of my heart, but all they did was use me, abuse me, manipulate me, and cause me even more pain. I now turn to you, Heavenly Father, asking you to fill every void in my life. Dig deep to touch and heal the hidden places in my heart that have haunted me for so long. I surrender my life unto you Lord. I give you total access to me.

Teach me how to trust you, teach me how to love you, and teach me how to let go of past experiences. Clear my mind of toxic memories. Give me the strength to disconnect from every person that is draining me and pulling me away from you. Help me to forgive my parents for everything they did or did not do that caused me pain. Take away the bitterness and replace it with total forgiveness. Renew my mind to understand that everything that has happened to me will work for my good. Continue to restore me, Lord, from the inside out. Fill me up with your love, power, presence, and guidance. No matter what I see, I know that with you, I am full. In Jesus' name, I pray. Amen.

READ WITH ME

Job 15:31   Psalm 63:1   Psalm 143:8

Joshua 1:9   Isaiah 40:31

CONNECT WITH ME

1. Is your glass half empty or half full, why?

2. What voids do you have from your childhood?

3. What area of your life do you need to be healed in? Have you tried Jesus?

4. Have you truly forgiven your parents for the part they played in your pain?

5. What are you going to do with this enlightenment?

REFLECTION

DAY 12:
VALIDATE ME, PLEASE

1. The action of checking or proving the validity or accuracy of something (*Merriam-Webster's Collegiate Dictionary*, 2015).

2. Recognition or affirmation that a person or their feelings or opinions are valid or worthwhile (*Merriam-Webster's Collegiate Dictionary*, 2015).

Here's my personal definition: *doing or saying something to prove to someone that you are who they will not acknowledge you as.*

      Have you ever been through or are you currently going through a stage in your life where you are seeking validation from others? Your constant craving for validation isn't for that of strangers you're seeking validation from people you love, people you look up to, and people whose opinions of you hold weight in your life. When these people fail to display their approval of you, it makes you feel like you aren't good enough to impress them, not working hard enough, or that you're not really as important to them as you thought you were.

      Let's say you play sports, and you just had the best game of your career. Everyone around you is celebrating your success and outstanding performance, but the only opinion that you're concerned about is the opinion of the person you're seeking validation from. It may be a fact that you just won the championship game, but the truth is you still feel like a loser. This tends to happen when you associate your success with validation from other people. Sometimes, from those who don't even have expertise in the area you've been successful in. For you, success is meeting the expectations of the people you love most.

Parents are often at the top of the "whose opinion matters the most" list for people of all ages. It's obvious why people who don't have great relationships with their parents seek validation from them— but what about the people who seem to have honorable parents? What about the parents that show up to most of their child's games, provide financial resources, and meet physical needs? These parents excel in the areas of providing, protecting, and teaching, but may lack the ability to openly express affection.

Although the child may have heard, "I love you," a few times, the child may have never heard the parent(s) speak on how important he/she is to them or how proud they are. The child secretly longs for their parents' words of affirmation concerning them. The parents' lack of providing mental, emotional, and spiritual nurturing causes the child to feel like they're not meeting the expectations of his/her parents. Because the parents never verbally confirm what the child means to them, the child spends his/her entire life seeking validation from not only the parents but from others.

Maybe your parents never told you how beautiful you are, so you look for validation of your beauty from men or other people. Maybe your parents said harsh and hurtful words to you, but never found their way around to apologize. So, now, you cling to people who are quick to say they're sorry without changed behavior, thus leading you to accept counterfeit apologies with ease. Are you saying to yourself, "well if they really thought I was beautiful, talented, or important then why didn't they just say it?"

Sometimes, parents or other important people in your life don't know that they are hurting you by not saying the things you want or need to hear. I know you may be thinking, "they're parents," or "they're adults so they should know what I need." Well, what if told you they actually don't know that you need words of affirmation or acts of affection to make you feel mentally, emotionally, and spiritually secure? Maybe they are unaware of these needs you desire because like you, they never received validation from those they loved and looked up to. I believe you would agree with me when I say that it's hard to do something well when you've never experienced it for yourself.

Let's talk about a baby for a moment. Several babies stop drinking from bottles when their 1-year-old birthday is near because they are soon to enter the toddler stage of their life. During the first couple of months of the baby's life, the mother held the baby's bottle for the baby while feeding. As the baby grew in age and size, the baby learned how to hold its own bottle to feed himself. Now, let's say the baby turns a year old and the mother takes the baby's bottle away. Although she knows the baby will not like this, the mother takes the bottle away because the baby has now grown into a toddler. The mother pours the toddler's milk into a sippy cup and hands the cup directly to the toddler. This time, the mother doesn't start off holding the cup for the toddler as she did with the bottle. She expects the toddler to know how to take the cup and turn it up to drink because the toddler is no longer considered a baby.

Drinking from the sippy cup requires the same motions that drinking from a bottle requires. Yet, the toddler cries in distress when the mother hands them the cup because the cup is unfamiliar, and the toddler hasn't been given any instructions or directions on how to use the cup. The mother wants the toddler to figure this task out on their own, so the mother doesn't step in to help. The toddler is thirsty and knows there is something to drink in the cup, so the toddler turns up the cup the best way he knows how and drinks from the cup. The cup may be upside down, turned backward, or spilling liquids all over the place, but none of that matters to the toddler at that moment. The toddler is satisfied with figuring out how to drink from their new sippy cup without any instructions or directions from mom.

Think of your parents as that new toddler and think of yourself as that new sippy cup. Although someone may have been there to help welcome you into your parent's lives, you were placed in your parent's arms with no directions or instructions. They may have seen other parents with children but watching is a lot easier than actually doing. Just like the toddler with its cup, your parents took what was given to them, which would be you, and did only what they knew best to do. Some toddlers catch on quickly, so they learn how to correctly drink from their cup on the first attempt. Some toddlers make several mistakes along the way but eventually, they learn how to drink from their cups correctly. And some toddlers have to give their cup back and drink from a bottle again because they cannot figure out how to handle the cup on their own.

  You are your parent's cup. Some parents were able to quickly catch on to the skills needed for parenthood. Some parents are making improvements along the way, and some parents had to pass you on to someone else to help care for you because they could not figure out how to be who you needed them to be. This is not making an excuse for your parents, but this will make forgiving them for their mistakes a little easier. This will also help you to overcome the feeling of needing to be validated by your parents or loved ones because of their lack of affection, attention, or presence in your life. Sometimes we look for validation from people who have no clue on how to give it.

  Let's switch gears. Maybe you're not seeking validation from your parents. Maybe you're seeking validation from friends, classmates, co-workers, or society in general. Social media apps, TV programs, and the World Wide Web all play a major part in your need to feel validated by others. Something as simple as posting a picture on a social media app… isn't actually so simple after all. You need the perfect angles, the perfect lighting, the perfect filter, and even the perfect background before you even consider uploading the photo online. I'm not saying that every picture you post is linked to your need to be validated. I'm sure there are several pictures you post simply because you like them. The problem comes in when you only receive a few likes or loves on a picture that you once felt amazing about. The lack of attention that your picture receives makes you feel unworthy, unloved and has you contemplating between deleting the picture or reposting the picture at a different time to see if the picture receives more reactions from others.

For you and many others, validation on social media is centered around likes, loves, shares, and retweets but I'm here to tell you that not receiving the attention you think you deserve from others isn't a direct indicator that your outfit or your hair wasn't cute in the picture you posted. Some of the people you're seeking validation from on social media secretly admire you from afar. They wish they look like you, dress like you, or have your personality. Their pride will never allow them to admit this, so instead of double tapping your picture or sharing a cute comment, they chose to ignore you or criticize you in an attempt to crush your self-confidence.

Listen to me and listen well! You don't need validation from anyone! You are who God says you are, and you are beautiful inside and out. You were created for such a time as this. The only validation you need is validation from God. The people that you're so desperately seeking validation from can't validate you because they did not call you to be who you are now. God did! Don't be so focused on receiving validation from others that you miss out on all of the wonderful things God has said about you.

From this day forth forget about seeking validation from people. Boldly and confidently live your life knowing you're beautiful, you're talented, you're important, you matter, you're smart, you're special, you will be successful, and knowing that I love you and God loves you. There is no one else on this earth exactly like you and your uniqueness is God's gift to this world. Although people you love may not admit these things, remember the words that God has already spoken to you in private concerning your future. One day, in His perfect timing, God is going to validate you publicly. When God validates you, people have no choice but to respect you for who you truly are.

PRAY WITH ME

Father God, thank you for this new outlook on my life. No longer will I seek validation from anyone except you. Lord, heal my heart of the pain that the people I love have caused me, known and unknown. Lord, give me strength where I am weak and boost my confidence in every area that I am lacking. I pray to never experience the feelings of abandonment, neglect, unworthiness, or low self-esteem in my life again. Lord, you are everything I need, and you are always here for me. Grant me the wisdom to understand the difference between real friends and people only pretending to be my friend. Help me to forgive those that didn't give me the love and affection I desired and forgive me for thinking I was alone when you were always here with me. From this day forth, I shall no longer complain or be depressed about the lack of validation from anyone. I know who God says that I am, and I know that God created me to do great and marvelous works in the world. In due time, I know that God will publicly validate me. I am whole, I am free, and I am filled with Joy. In Jesus' name, I pray, amen.

READ WITH ME

Psalm 68:5   1 Peter 2:9   Galatians 6:9   1 Peter 2:9

CONNECT WITH ME

1. Who are you seeking validation from?

2. Why do you feel the need to be validated by that person or those people?

3. How would forgiving those that have caused you pain or discomfort help you heal?

4. What does Psalm 68:5 say and how does this make you feel?

REFLECTION

DAY 13:
GIRL, WASH YOUR FACE

Makeup has been around for centuries. Women wear makeup for several different reasons, but I believe the most common reasons are to enhance their beauty and to cover blemishes, scars, and imperfections. Even if you don't wear makeup, I'm sure at some point in your life you've encountered another female that does. For this devotional, we're going to use some makeup tools and products as spiritual representations. Similar to a mask, makeup can be used to create an illusion of what a person feels is more acceptable or pleasing to the reflection of themselves or to the view of others. I'm no makeup artist, but I want you to go on a 'face beat" journey with me.

Foundation

Think about this for a moment: when building or creating something, the foundation is most important because the foundation affects everything built on top of it. Many women apply foundation to their face first as a base covering. The foundation that you put on your face will affect every other product that will be applied on top of it. You apply foundation to your face because it creates a nice, smooth, and even skin tone. By definition, a person's tone reflects their mood, spirit, character, and attitude.

The type of foundation you use is based on what product you feel blends your uneven skin tone the best. The amount of foundation you use depends on how flawed you feel your skin tone is. If you take a spiritual look at your face, you will find that you apply foundation to cover your true tone. In this case, your spiritual tone is actually your true feelings. The feelings you pretend not to have. The feelings that have been hurt, damaged, and manipulated. The feelings that you've learned to mask. You've hidden the root causes of these feelings under your foundation to create an illusion that your tone is smooth and radiant. When really, it's filled with blotches of pain, manipulation, confusion, and unforgiveness. While foundation can cover most of those faint blemishes, you need a concealer to cover the dark circles, scars, and major areas of discolorations.

Concealer

Spiritually, you use concealer to cover up the major damages caused by toxic relationships. Whether it was relationships from partners, parents, siblings, friends, or ministry, these relationships produced wounds that eventually closed, but left you with scars. The words that were spoken against your name and character by people you trusted; the names that you were called by people you love; the way they doubted you when you told them your dreams and visions; the way they hated on you after you put in work and God manifested great things in your life; the lies they told on you because they were jealous of who you were becoming; the way they turned their back on you when you needed them most; the way they misused, abused, and cheated on you when all you tried to do was show them love; the way they belittled your gifts and talents; all of these scars you mask with concealer.

Mascara

Physically, you apply mascara to darken, thicken, or lengthen your eyelashes due to thinness and/or shortness. Mascara's overall goal is to make your eyelashes appear to be longer than they really are. Spiritually, your mascara is lengthening the things that you feel come up short in your life such as relationships, self-esteem, joy, happiness, peace of mind, and confidence.

Eyelashes

Although eyelashes can put an emphasis on beauty, their primary role is to protect your eyes from dust, dirt, or any other small particles trying to enter your eyes. Lashes also help tell your eyelids when they need to close to keep harmful things from entering your eyes. Spiritually, you feel your lashes weren't efficient at their job because some bad things did in fact gain access to your eyes.

Was it the physical abuse you saw as a child? Was it the way you saw your mother allow men to treat her that confused you on how a man should treat you? Was it the sexual acts that someone prematurely exposed you to that caused your innocent eyes to become entangled into a world that you weren't ready to experience? Or was it your environment that caused you to hate who you were because you wanted to live the life of others that seemed to be happier, wealthier, and better off than you? Whatever your personal reason is, it makes you feel like your lashes always came up short, so you added an extra set of lashes to your own. In your mind, although you cannot unsee what you've already seen, you can try to control what you see next.

Blush

When I think of creating vibrant-colored cheeks, it gives an impression of excitement. Blush: its name pretty much speaks for itself. The spiritual blush that you wear on your face represents all of the counterfeit men and boys that used their slick talk and deceitful ways to manipulate you into "blushing" and falling for them.

Highlights

Highlights are applied to your face to create a special glow in addition to all of the other products that have been used. It brings about a particular focus on the area it has been applied to, giving you a bright and attention-filled finish. Your spiritual highlights create a glow and concentration on all of the mistakes you've made in the past. The things you've done wrong that you're too embarrassed to admit to; the shameful acts you participated in that only you and God know about; the things that the devil tries to use against you to make you feel like you're not worthy of God's grace and mercy. The devil highlights these things in an attempt to keep you from becoming totally healed and free.

Lip Stick

Women wear lipstick for several different reasons, one of which would be to enhance the appearance of that particular area. Women use many different shades and colors of lipstick to draw attention to their lips, for it is said that the lips are a sensual part of the body that many men are attracted to. When applying spiritual lipstick, I think of highlighting the area of the face that is connected to the most powerful tool on the entire body: the tongue. This is dressed up with many colors, shades, and coats because like in the physical, it is pleasing to the eyes of others.

Spiritual lipstick represents all of the word curses spoken against your name by others and it even represents the words of doubt you've spoken about yourself. The words that come from these lips are a major part of the reason you have been bound for so long. Death and life lie in the power of the tongue; the verse mentions *death* first probably because sometimes, as humans, we are more inclined to speak negatively than positively. But you have the power to choose!

You've masked your face with so much spiritual makeup that it has become a spiritual weight that you're carrying around. You're bigger, you're stronger, you're wiser and more mature than ever before. It's time to stop masking the things you've been through and own who you really are. You are not what you went through... you are the beauty of surviving. Under that mask is a beautiful, strong, woman of God. They tried to bury you, but what they did not know is you are a seed destined to grow. On today, I dare you to release every spiritual makeup layer you're wearing and to create fresh, fertile ground for your seed to grow on. Girl, Go Wash Your Face!

READ WITH ME

Isaiah 54:17   Romans 8:28   Psalm 51: 10-19
Proverbs 18:21   Matthew 16:18   Hebrews 12:1-2

PRAY WITH ME

    Father God, I come humbly as I know how to say thank you for your goodness and mercy. Thank you for the correction, protection, and experiences that you've helped me survive thus far. I know that all things work together for my good, so I trust that every hidden pain in my heart will be healed through your perfect love. You knew that I would survive my painful past, so you allowed me to go through it because it is in my getting through that I will be able to help someone else. Some weight that I carried was never a part of your plan, but it was my own selfish ambitions that cost me some sleepless nights and weary days. I tried to mask my pain for so long. I walked around like everything was okay when I was dying on the inside.

    But on today, I lay every weight of my past at your feet. I trade my yoke for yours for your yoke is much lighter. Heal me, change me, and renew me from the inside out. Tear down the walls that I've put up and build me on a new solid foundation. I forgive those that have caused me pain and I forgive myself for resting in the place of a victim instead of walking in victory. I forgive so that I too can be forgiven by you, Lord. No weapon formed against me shall prosper and every tongue that rises against me in judgment, I condemn. On today, I choose to be free, I choose to be healed, and I choose to be happy. On today, I choose you, God. Cover me with your blood; cover me with your grace and mercy. Strengthen me to walk in my new identity in you. Give me the courage to walk into the unknown assured that you've already ordered my steps. I submit to your will and your way. Baptize me, Lord, in your holy name. In Jesus' name, I pray, Amen.

CONNECT WITH ME

1. What are you wearing spiritually? Are you masking your pain under fake happiness?

2. Dig deep, and peel back every layer of pain that you've masked even from your childhood. List the people, places, and things that hurt you.

3. Who are you under the mask? Who do you want to be? What is holding you back?

4. What scripture from today's reading has helped you to remove your mask and how?

REFLECTION

DAY 14:
NO BOAZ? THAT'S RUTH'S MAN, ANYWAY

Lord, where is my Boaz? I'm waiting for Boaz to find me! Lord, when is my Boaz coming?

Well, I hate to be the bearer of bad news, in this case not really, but GIRL HE AIN'T COMING! That's Ruth's man anyway! One of the most popular bible stories preached and told to single women is the story of Ruth. If you are not familiar with this story, it is a fairly quick read. Take a moment to read the book of Ruth, then return to this devotional. It's a beautiful love story about a widow minding her own business, taking care of her widowed mother-in-law, and working when she is suddenly swept off her feet by this wealthy, respectful, hardworking man who just so happens to be her boss. They marry, have a son, and live happily ever after. This quick summary of the story explains why Ruth is the ultimate go-to story when someone is attempting to encourage single women to wait for a good man to find them.

I'm going to take a different approach when discussing this story with you. It is not impossible for your love story to play out the way Ruth's story did, but it's important for you not to put your primary focus on the arrival of Boaz in Ruth's life. Of course, Boaz plays a significant role in the story, but the book is named "Ruth," not "When Ruth meets Boaz."

Let's focus on what Ruth was doing in order to be in the position for Boaz to find her. The first thing Ruth did was remain loyal. Not only did she remain loyal to her mother-in-law after the death of Ruth's husband, but Ruth also remained loyal to God by choosing to stay and serve God because He was not the god of her family's culture. Ruth remained loyal to a God that seemed to have forsaken her with the death of her husband, brother-in-law, and father-in-law. How loyal are you? Do you remain at God's feet when things aren't going your way, or do you have temper tantrums and run away from God?

    The next thing Ruth did was serve and work. Ruth served her mother-in-law wholeheartedly without complaining. Ruth physically went out and found work in order to care for her mother-in-law and herself. Ruth's focus was never on finding a husband but instead, she focused on serving and working. Are you working? Not just for income, but are you working on your dreams, your goals, and your visions? Ruth was able to receive advice from her mother-in-law, follow instructions given to her, and remain patient, which ultimately led to the marriage of her and Boaz. Can you receive wisdom from others, or do you think you already know everything? Are you able to see things from others' points of view or is it your way or no way?

    Boaz can be a representation of the man God has for you just as Ruth can be a representation of what you should be doing in order to be found by the man God has for you. Stop looking for and waiting on Boaz to fly in like Superman to your rescue: that's Ruth's man! When looking at Boaz in the story, take your focus off of who Boaz is physically and place your focus on his characteristics, morals, and values. It is these things that you should use as a guide when deciding if a man has been sent to you by God.

    When you're single, it's easy to see a "Boaz," or another woman's husband that's being good to her, and begin to think, "I want one of those," or "I want a relationship like that." You see the way he treats his "Ruth," his wife, and you long for that type of love, but did you ever stop to think about what the wife had to do to get who and what she has now? What I want you to get from this devotional is that as a single woman, you have to let go of the literal fantasy of "Boaz" finding you. The man God has just for you should have characteristics, morals, and values similar to Boaz; your love story may or may not play out the way Ruth's did, but understand that God will never send you somebody else's man! Your focus needs to be on becoming more like Ruth in order to receive a love similar to the one she gained. Loyalty, serving, working, being able to accept direction, willingly following instructions, and having patience will not get you Boaz, but it will get you the man God has made just for you in God's perfect timing.

READ WITH ME

Ruth 1:1-22   Ruth 2:1-23
Ruth 3:1-18   Ruth 4:1-22

PRAY WITH ME

Father God, in the mighty name of Jesus, I come to you saying thank you. Thank you for the revelation and a new outlook on my season of waiting. Show me myself, Lord. Clear my mind of any memories of ungodly relationships and fantasies. Help me to shift my focus from being found by a man to being in a deeper relationship with you. Show me how to seek your face; teach me how to love you. I want to know you like never before because I know it is in finding your love that I will find the courage to love myself. Remove every lustful spirit that attempts to confuse my mind and heart. Help me be patient while waiting for your perfect timing. Teach me how to wait diligently. Help me focus on working harder. Help me to focus on becoming wiser and stronger. Show me where I lack discipline and ambition. Give me new ideas to push my dreams to a greater level. Help me to be more like Ruth in loyalty, faith, serving, and humility. Teach me how to serve you better. In Jesus' name, I pray, Amen.

CONNECT WITH ME

1. Are you waiting on Boaz or are you waiting on the man God has for you?

2. What are you doing to prepare for the arrival of the man you desire?

3. What are your goals, dreams, and visions?

4. In what ways are you being productive while you are waiting on your significant other?

5. Are you willing to serve God and others while waiting? How?

REFLECTION

DAY 15:
UNTIE THE KNOT

Soul tie- an inner connection (biological and spiritual) between two or more human beings produced by sexual intercourse and sometimes relationships not involving sexual contact.

I've been pretty transparent throughout this book and I want to keep it that way. The "sex talk" and "relationship talk" between adults and young adults can be some of the most awkward, embarrassing, and uncomfortable conversations to have for some, while others find the conversation to be simple, educating, and natural. Whether you had a good experience or a bad experience with this conversation in the past, I would like to have this conversation with you. As the definition stated at the beginning, there are two different types of soul ties: relational soul ties and sexual soul ties. A relational soul tie is established through close friendships and relationships between two individuals, while a sexual soul tie is established through sexual intercourse between two individuals.

Let's dig into relational soul ties first. Every relationship a person is in has occurred through kinship, marriage, conversations, recreations, or spiritual connections. Some relationships are beneficial, and some are detrimental. It is extremely important for you to thoroughly and truthfully evaluate every relationship you're in. Take a moment and ask yourself this question: "what relationships am I involved in that are causing me more pain than joy?" Remember, being honest with yourself is one of the best things you could ever do for yourself. Attitudes, emotions, and mindsets are contagious when you're around someone for extended periods of time. You can begin to pick up on their habits and actions without even realizing it. Some people have good habits you pick up and some people have bad habits you will pick up. The same way certain types of foods you consume have an effect on your natural health is the same way different types of spirits you consume have an effect on your spiritual health.

When you're in a relationship with someone, it is much like the relationship a chef has with a guest dining in their restaurant. Because the chef is the person in charge of cooking or creating the food, the chef is also in charge of what his guest will eat. Of course, the guest will be able to choose the meal of their liking from a menu, but regardless of which meal the guest chooses to order, the moment the guest chose to eat at that particular restaurant was the moment the chef was given power over the meal the guest will consume.

Every chef doesn't prepare meals the same way. The ingredients a chef uses and how they use them is what makes the chef unique from other chefs. Every person you're in a relationship with, including friendship, is like a chef in your life, and you're the guest eating from their restaurant. Every person you're in a relationship with feeds you from their kitchen. Their kitchen is their heart. You can't see a person's heart when you're standing next to them because it's hidden inside their body. You can't see a chef's kitchen because it's hidden inside their restaurant. Meals are prepared privately in their kitchen. You don't get to see what goes on in the kitchen while the chef is preparing your meal, but the kitchen is the place from which the food the chef plans to feed you will come.

Luke 6:45 NIV says, "a good man brings good things out of the good stored up in his heart, and an evil man brings evil things out of the evil stored up in his heart. For the mouth speaks what the heart is full of." You can't physically see what goes on in the heart of the people you're in a relationship with, but a hint about what goes on in their heart is the type of "food" they prepare for you to consume. A chef that only feeds their guest junk food or undercooked food is like the person that only feeds you bad news, gossip, or toxic suggestions. Hold on, before you start bashing the chef, let's self-reflect. Remember, you are a guest that has the ability to simply get up and walk out of the restaurant if you are not satisfied with the meal that has been prepared for you. But keep in mind, you can't eat all of what's been served then decide to walk out of the restaurant without paying. If you choose to remain in a relationship that is toxic, don't get upset when it's time to pay for what you indulged in. You have a choice of what you're going to eat and where you are going to eat from. There are some places you've been eating from and some people that you've been eating with that have been feeding your flesh but starving your soul. My advice to you is to go on a spiritual diet.

    Now, let's talk about the more commonly known soul tie, the sexual soul tie. Everyone has different methods of teaching or sharing knowledge on this topic. Depending upon the source from which you received your knowledge, you may still have some unanswered questions or lingering thoughts about sexual soul ties. No matter who you had the "sex talk" with, more than likely, the conversation ended somewhere along the lines of "don't have sex until you're married," or "if you have sex, use protection." If you're anything like I was, you're curious to know why you were told those things. "Because I said so," just didn't cut it for me in this conversation. I'm sure you've heard about all of the STDs you can contract through sex and about the risk of pregnancy. These are definitely major and valid reasons not to engage in sex until marriage. When you engage in sexual intercourse with another individual, there is a spiritual exchange that takes place. During intercourse, individuals exchange emotions, energies, DNA, and hormones. Whether you use protection or not, this process still takes place spiritually and once you have sexually connected with a person, you are bound together as one. What I mean by this is: you're pretty much marrying the person you're having sex with, not physically, but spiritually. When two people get married, they're bonded together forever unless they're legally separated. If that isn't already a tough pill to swallow, know that when you have sexual intercourse with a person not only are you creating a soul tie with them, but you're also creating a soul tie with every individual that person had sex with before you and the people that they had sex with, and whoever those people had sex with, and the list just goes on. It's a domino effect. Can you imagine being married and tied to so many people? People that you don't even know? Sexual intercourse causes you to gain or have an increase of feelings of affection, closeness, lust, attachment, compassion, and admiration for the person you've connected with. In other words, it causes you to fall in love. But what happens if the relationship doesn't work out or the person you had sex with doesn't want to be in a relationship with you? The obvious: heartbreak. Sure, you can fall in love with someone without having sex with them, but the pain that a heartbreak causes is excruciating no matter the circumstance.

It takes time to heal a broken heart and when you add a soul tie to the equation the healing process becomes much more complicated. Imagine yourself holding onto a rope. The rope represents the person you're in love with. When the relationship ends or the person no longer wishes to be held on to by you, you are stuck with the painful task of letting go of the rope. Letting go isn't always easy, especially when you've planned a future with that person, you've created countless memories with that person, and you've gotten comfortable having them in your life. When you gain your strength and finally decide to let go of the person you were madly in love with, all you have to do is let go of the rope and you can walk away in freedom.

Now, let's say you had sexual intercourse with the person you were in love with, and you've finally gotten to the point where you're ready to let go of the rope. This time when you let the rope go, the rope doesn't just fall down as you walk away. Unlike before when you dropped the rope and walked away in freedom, this time when you drop the rope and walk away the rope is still there, tied to your wrist. The person on the other end of the rope is walking away and pulling you right along with them because you created a soul tie with them through sexual intercourse. You want to be free of them, you want to move on with your life, you want to be happy again and find true love, but no matter how hard you try it seems like something keeps pulling you back. You can't keep your mind off of them, you don't even like their personality anymore, but something just makes you want to go back. That "something" is a soul tie.

Maybe you did manage to move on to a new relationship, but you're noticing your attitude, patience, desires, and emotions have changed drastically. You don't feel like yourself, but you can't seem to figure out why. The "why" can be because of soul ties from the person you were previously with and also all of the people they've been with. Moving on to a new relationship doesn't cancel old soul ties, it only adds another rope to your wrist along with the one you already have. Trying to untie a knot isn't easy and neither is being delivered from a soul tie. You will need assistance from your spiritual leaders, prayer, fasting, and whatever else the process of being delivered from soul ties requires.

As you take into consideration the side effects of being in a relationship with someone and having sexual intercourse with someone, I pray that you understand the importance and benefits of waiting until you're married to have sex. If you have already crossed that threshold, it's okay, you're not totally doomed. If you desire, you can be set free and redeemed of your previous actions. God is faithful and forgiving. There's nothing too big for God to handle. Remember, some packages are better left unopened until you're prepared to handle the consequences and weight of what's inside.

READ WITH ME

1 Corinthians 6:15-20   Galatians 5:1   Hebrews 13:4

1 Corinthians 6:9-18   1 John 1-9   1 Thessalonians 4:3-5

PRAY WITH ME

Dear Heavenly Father, thank you for the knowledge and wisdom that you've allowed me to gain on today. Thank you for loving me enough to correct my unsettling behaviors and curiosity. Lord, I ask that you help me make mature and wise decisions daily. Control my eyes, control my hormones, control my emotions, Lord, for I'm only human and I can't do these things alone. Lord, protect me from lustful spirits and people that attempt to manipulate my mind. Give me the strength and courage to say "NO" to sex outside of marriage. Open my eyes so that I can see who my real friends are and those that really love and care for me.

Reveal to me the intentions of those that come to deceive me, hurt me, and use me. Lord, give me strength over peer pressure and give me confidence in myself to know that I don't have to be like the people around me to be cool. Heal my heart of all scars and pain from my past experiences. Free my mind of memories from toxic relationships and situations that were not ordained by you. I repent of my sins and I give my mind, heart, body, and soul to you, Lord. I shall live to please you. In Jesus' Name, I Pray, Amen.

CONNECT WITH ME

1. After reading this devotional, are there any friendships or relationships that you need to walk away from?

2. What are the benefits of not connecting sexually with people outside of marriage?

3. Can you be tangled in a soul tie without sexual relations with someone?

4. How can you become free from a soul tie?

5. What does 1 Thessalonians 4:3-5 tell you?

REFLECTION

DAY 16:
MUTUAL DISCONNECT

"So if the Son sets you free, you will be free indeed" (John 8:36, NIV)

When God has set you free, don't forfeit your freedom by keeping in touch with bondage through mutual connections. Ever heard of the saying "break up with the whole family?" This is where breakups can get tricky because when the relationship is over, more than likely, you established bonds and connections with your ex's family members and immediate circle. Whether it's mama, sister, grandma, auntie, cousins, friends, whatever the case may be, it is crucial that you take time to be totally free and disconnected from those that are mutually connected to your ex.

Now I know you're thinking, "well that's not fair, they didn't do anything to me, my ex did," or "I was friends with them before I got involved with my ex." I understand your point of view because it was once my own, but I want you to take a moment and meditate on this new point of view I'm presenting to you. Understand that by keeping an open connection with his family members or people closest to him, you're leaving a door open for the enemy to have access to you through these mutual connections. The enemy comes to kill, steal, and destroy. He doesn't care who he uses or how he uses them to get to you as long as he completes his mission.

Think about the social network Facebook. On this platform, whether your profile is set to private or public, there is a feature on Facebook called "mutual friends", which informs the viewer if they have any mutual friends with you. There is a way to set your friend list to private so that your entire list will be hidden from anyone viewing your page, but mutual friends are always visible. Although you can control who sees the content on your page, you cannot control who sees your mutual friend list. Your mutual friend list will always show what friends you and the viewer have in common. Mutual friends create access. No matter how private you set out to be, a mutual connection between an ex's family members and friends will create a door of access to you. This doesn't mean you have to hate them; it doesn't mean you're mad at them; neither does it mean you don't love them anymore. You simply cannot heal in the same environment you were hurt in. Total healing is going to require you to love yourself enough to disconnect from people and reconnect to God. If the mutual connection really cares about you, they will respect and honor your decision to disconnect from them while you heal.

    It's always harder to see the amount of damage a storm has caused while the storm is going on. Once the storm is over and you appraise the aftermath, you can see things for what they really are because, at this point, you no longer have to make rash decisions based on emotional trauma. It is in the moments of trying to recover some things that belonged to you before the storm hit, that you realize what seemed to only be a rain shower was actually a hurricane.

    The significant thing about hurricanes is they always have a couple more "mutual friends" called tropical storms hanging around. These tropical storms usually don't make landfall, but weather specialists always warn us to keep an eye out for tropical storms because they will cause us to experience some climate changes such as strong winds, heavy rains, and flooding. Your ex was the hurricane in your life that caused the most damage, but those mutual friends and family members are the lingering tropical storms. They won't cause as much damage as the hurricane, but you will experience some climate changes that will affect your property. Your property represents your peace, joy, happiness, memory, emotions, and mental capacity. This is why it's so important to foreclose (disconnect) your property as you rebuild (heal). I know it's a tough thing to do, but in your time of disconnection, God will reveal to you those that really love and care about you and those that were only connected to you to keep the storm going.

PRAY WITH ME

Dear Heavenly Father, thank you for opening my eyes today to see beyond the counterfeits and storms in my life. I pray that you reveal to me every snake in the grass and every person secretly praying on my downfall. Lord, give me the strength to cut ties with those that are using me and keeping me in bondage. Close my ears to toxic advice and ill-willed conversations. Free me of soul ties from every unordained connection. Heal my heart and rest my mind from the torment of false possibilities. Help me to release the pain that's buried deep within my heart from past relationships and situations.

Give me the wisdom and the knowledge on how to go forth with my life in power and freedom. No longer shall I be bound by mutual connections and their hidden agendas. Detour every hurricane and tropical storm that is headed my way and if I'm already in a storm, help me to see my way through the recovery process. Today, I proclaim that I am free! Free of bondage, guilt, shame, pain, and unauthorized connections. Praise the Lord, I'm free! Thank You, Lord, for your divine protection. In Jesus' name, I pray, Amen.

READ WITH ME

John 8:36   Genesis 3:1-20   Mark 4:35-41

John 10:9-10   2 Corinthians 6:14-16

CONNECT WITH ME

1. What relationship have you been freed from or what relationship do you desire to be free from?

2. What mutual connections are associated with this relationship?

3. What are the benefits of disconnecting from mutual connections? Do you need to disconnect temporarily or permanently and why?

4. What does "freedom" mean for you and how do you gain it?

REFLECTION

DAY 17:
COMFORT ZONE

It was a Thursday afternoon and I'd finally made it home from a long day of work. Earlier that day, I created a schedule for myself to follow in order to complete a project that was due the next day. The plan was to come home, take a shower, eat dinner, complete my household tasks, and then focus on completing the project that I had been pushing aside for an entire week. I sat down at my study table, opened my laptop, and began to work on the project. I diligently worked from the table for fifteen minutes, but I soon noticed how uncomfortable my body felt sitting in my chair at the table.

    I knew I focused better at the table, but I decided that being comfortable was more important than staying where I knew I worked best. I knew my tablet was capable of allowing me to complete my project, so I shut down my laptop, picked up my tablet, and sat cross-legged on my bed. I could've used my laptop while sitting on my bed, but my tablet allowed me to rest in a more comfortable position. My bed is more comfortable than the chair at the table, so when I sat on my bed in an attempt to work on my project, my body became relaxed. I sat on my bed working from my tablet for ten minutes before my body began to feel uncomfortable again. I convinced myself that since my phone was much lighter than my tablet, I would be most comfortable lying down while completing the project from my phone.

    My phone had the same capabilities as my laptop and tablet, so why not give it a shot? Well, five minutes into lying down and working on my project from my phone, my body became so relaxed that I drifted off to sleep. I was awakened by my alarm clock the next morning with no time to complete my project. There was only time for me to get dressed for work and regret my decisions from the previous night.

Procrastination was the first thing I did wrong. Waiting to complete something hours, minutes, or moments before it's due leaves you no time to meditate on corrections or adjustments needed to fulfill the task at hand. Not following through with my plan was my second mistake. Although I started out in the order that I planned, I began to steer away from my plan when I began to listen to my feelings rather than my mind. I knew I worked most efficiently on my laptop at my study table, but my body showed signs of discomfort because it wanted to relax.

Instead of continuing to work from the position that would give me the best results, I compromised the completion of my project for my body's demand for comfort. Each time my body felt uncomfortable sitting in a certain position, I moved to a new position in an attempt to satisfy my body's demands. I thought moving to a more comfortable position would make my body's demands stop, but instead, my body continued to demand more comfort until I fell asleep. My body wasn't totally comfortable until I was in a position of total rest. I had purchased comfort at the expense of an incomplete project. None of the positions I was working in were causing my body any kind of hurt, harm, or danger. My body produced feelings of discomfort because its plan was to get my mind to agree with my feelings and allow myself to relax. Relaxation leads to rest and sleep.

Sometimes, God or people with authority over you such as parents, bosses, coaches, or teachers, can place you in uncomfortable positions. Your parent(s) may require you to complete homework before enjoying electronics or require you to complete your chores before going to a friend's house. Your boss may require you to submit paperwork before clocking out. Your coach may require you to run extra laps for mistakes made during games. Your teacher may require you to attend tutoring sessions during the summer months to help you better prepare for the upcoming school year. God may require you to stay at a place of having just enough financially because He knows you'll never move from your current position if you become comfortable with the wages that career offers. It gets frustrating when you are required to do uncomfortable things. There is nothing wrong with wanting to do things that make you feel good, but I want you to understand that everything that is comfortable isn't always going to give the best results.

Instead of getting upset with God or others for pushing you out of your comfort zone, remember that growth takes place in uncomfortable situations. If you're always comfortable that means you're not growing and if you're not growing that means you're resting in stagnation. If you're stagnant, you're not making any progress towards your desired destination. I don't know about you, but I want to grow so that I can accomplish my goals and reach my dreams. Most importantly, I want to grow so that I can become exactly who God called me to be.

PRAY WITH ME

Lord, thank you for placing people of authority in my life to teach me, love me, guide me, train me, and care for me. Even if I feel like the people that should be doing these things are not living up to my expectations, Lord, I thank you for filling every void and being everything I need. Lord, help me become a better listener. Forgive me, Lord, for not always putting my best into everything that I do. Help me become a better daughter, sister, aunt, friend, and leader. Help me to receive instructions and corrections in love. Lord, help me to become a more diligent worker and remove all thoughts and temptations of procrastination out of my life. Lord give me the wisdom to understand the power of submission and obedience. As I continue to grow, Lord grant me the wisdom, strength, courage, and humility I need to be who you called me to be. In Jesus' name, I pray, Amen.

READ WITH ME

Hebrews 12:11 Galatians 6:9
1 Peter 3:17 Hebrews 13:17

CONNECT WITH ME

1. What's pushing you out of your comfort zone?

2. What can you do differently to avoid procrastination?

3. What does Hebrews 12:11 say about being pushed into uncomfortable positions?

4. What does Hebrews 13:17 say about listening to and receiving instructions from those that have been ordained to have authority over you?

REFLECTION

DAY 18:
I CAN DO ANYTHING BETTER THAN YOU

"Mastering a skill requires being led, guided, or mentored through correction, conviction, and connections by someone who is more experienced than you or someone who has already mastered the skill you're learning." -Chantoria Scott

    The journey you're on to the destiny God has planned for your life isn't always easy. In fact, I think it's safe to say that the journey gets hard sometimes. As you move further along on your journey, you will continue to experience elevation. Based on a student's overall performance during a particular time frame, a teacher has the ability to promote a student to the next grade level or retain the student to repeat the same grade level. In order to qualify for promotion to the next grade level, the student must be able to prove to the teacher they've mastered all of the skills that have been demonstrated. When the student's work reflects mastery, then, and only then, will the student's elevation to the next grade level take place. The only way a student can reach mastery level is to be instructed by a teacher.

    Personally, I'm a student and a teacher in my profession. How ironic is that? My favorite phrase to tell people when they ask me about my teaching career is, "I'm a teacher second, I'm a student first." An effective teacher must be a student first. Quick tip for you on your journey of elevation: don't be so quick to want to lead because even the leader must be willing to follow. I think you'll agree that one of the hardest parts about being a student is when your teacher has taught you their method of obtaining an accurate answer to an equation, but you've figured out your own method that's faster than the method the teacher taught you. Your method gives you the same answer that your teacher has, but the teacher will not give you credit for your work because you did not follow their method to solve the equation. That has to be the most unfair thing ever, right? The answers are the same, so who cares about what method was used as long as the final answer is correct?

Believe me, I know the feeling, but let me talk to you from a teacher's perspective. In most cases, the reason your teacher wants you to use their method of problem-solving is that they've already mastered the level you're currently on. They know that you're going to need the method they've taught you to be able to complete the work you're going to encounter on the next grade level. While the method you used may have given you an accurate answer for that particular problem, it is not the answer that the teacher is concerned about. It's the ability to operate the problem-solving method they've taught you.

The method that the teacher wants you to master is only one piece of a larger puzzle. Mastering your teacher's class requires you to master the methods they've taught. When you elevate to the next grade level, you're going to need to use the problem-solving strategies you previously learned to take the new pieces of the puzzle your new teacher is going to hand you and build onto the pieces you've already put together. Simply knowing the answer will not help you on the next level. Mastering the skills needed to solve the problem is what will qualify you for the promotion.

When I was younger, I had chores to do in the house. The chore that I despised the most was washing dishes. My mother's method of washing dishes felt like torture at the time. First, you have to rinse the sink out to be sure it's clean and ready to wash the dirty dishes. So, clean the sink just to put something else dirty in the sink. Then, you have to put on the special dish-washing gloves. Next, you have to put the water stopper in the sink and begin to fill the sink with hot water. While the water is running, you have to add just enough dish soap to make a soapy solution. Adding too much soap would make the sink overflow with bubbles. After that, you must add 1 to 2 caps full of bleach to the soapy water. Now, you can finally start washing the dishes. Once you've washed and rinsed all of the dishes and neatly placed them in the draining rack, let the water out of the sink, clear out all the bubbles, squeeze out your dishrag and wipe the entire sink clean.

    Now, it's time to take your gloves off and hang them on the rack to dry. As if that's not already enough, next you have to get the drying towel and finish drying all of the dishes on the drying rack and put them away in the cabinets where they belong. The thing that frustrated me most about washing dishes using my mother's method was the fact that we had a brand new dishwasher in our kitchen, but my mother refused to let me use it because she thought her method of washing dishes was better and more effective than that of the dishwasher. I cringed every time I hand-washed dishes while looking at that brand new dishwasher. The dishwasher provided a new and faster method for washing dishes. All you had to do was load the dishes, put a detergent pack inside, close the door, press a button, then bam, all of the dishes were washed, dried, and ready to be put away in the cabinets. I told myself over and over that when I owned my own home, there would be a dishwasher in the kitchen, and I would use it!

    And when I got my first apartment, I did just that. It all was going great until one day, my dishwasher broke. I was upset for a moment, but I soon found myself using the method that my mother taught me. When I finished cleaning the dishes, I thought about all of the times I hated using the handwashing method when I was younger. It didn't feel good, it didn't make sense, and there were faster ways to wash dishes, yet my mother insisted that I use her method. It wasn't until years later when my dishwasher broke, that I appreciated the method my mother taught me. Because I was a master of the skills needed to wash dishes, I was able to complete the task using a different method. I became a master at dishwashing by learning my mother's method that I thought was old, useless, and outdated. One day, your method may not work, but as long as you've mastered the skill, you'll always be able to find another method.

You may know faster, smarter, and easier methods than those that your teacher has taught you, but you don't know everything just yet. Discovering other methods that work proves you have the potential to become even more advanced than your teacher, but potential only turns into talent after you have mastered all skills. Learn the skill before you expose the talent. Sometimes, God shows you a glimpse of your potential. If you are not careful, you can mistake your potential for your reality and try to skip the process it takes to turn potential into reality. Potential shows the capacity one has to develop into something or someone in the future.

Potential is not a definite destination; it is a glimpse of destiny guaranteed to be reached only if you complete the sequential, developmental process required to master skills and to be able to turn them into efficient talents. This applies to teachers, mothers, fathers, godmothers, godfathers, coaches, mentors, pastors, and any other person the Lord has assigned as a leader in your life. The point of being a student isn't to prove that your answers are correct, but, instead, to gain knowledge and master your teacher's methods so, in the future, you can build new methods on top of the ones you've already mastered.

PRAY WITH ME

Dear Heavenly Father, thank you for being the greatest teacher I could ever have. Thank you for the teachers you've placed in my life to help me grow spiritually, mentally, physically, and emotionally. Whether it's through my parents, a mentor, teacher, or pastor, I pray that you continue to pour knowledge, wisdom, and love into them, so in return, they will pour those things back into me. Lord, guard my mind and my heart from manipulators and counterfeits attempting to stop me from reaching my destiny as I travel on this journey of elevation.

Lord, keep me humble in my process of maturing and elevating. Help me to remember that I'm not greater than my teacher, but I shall humbly strive to be greater than those before me in your perfect timing. Help me to be submissive, respectful, and appreciative towards those that you have given authority over me. I pray for each teacher, leader, parent, and mentor in my life. I pray that they're obedient to your instructions on leading me and that they operate in love and kindness according to your will and your way. You never told me the journey would be easy, but I trust that you will be with me through my entire process. In Jesus' name, I pray, Amen.

READ WITH ME

| Proverbs 1:7 | Proverbs 4:6-7 | Proverbs 13:1 |
| James 1:5 | Proverbs 19:20. | Luke 6:40 |

CONNECT WITH ME

1. What is your role as a student? What is your teacher's role? Remember your teacher can be a pastor, teacher, parent, etc.

2. In what ways could you be a better student in school and in life?

3. What do the scriptures say about wisdom?

REFLECTION

DAY 19:
GPS, WHERE TO NEXT?

Anytime you're traveling alone to a new destination you'll find yourself needing some sort of GPS device to give you directions. Along your journey of elevation, you're going to need a GPS to give you directions to your final destination. Thankfully, you're equipped with the best GPS available: God's Perfect Strategy. Maybe you've created your own plans for your life. You've mapped out the type of house you will live in, the type of career path you will pursue, the places you will visit, and the things you will do in your spare time. Having a plan is essential to your overall success, but it's the strategy that will steer you to your destination. If you have a plan but no strategy, then you're just wandering aimlessly.

There will come a point in your life when God will wreck the plans that you've made for yourself because those plans aren't a part of his perfect strategy for your life. As you mature and grow don't be surprised when some of the plans you had for your life begin to change. Some of the things you use to enjoy doing like partying and getting drunk will no longer give you a thrill. Some of the friends you planned on having in your life forever are going to fade away. That school or college you planned on attending didn't accept you or you couldn't afford the tuition rate, so it caused you to become an ineligible student. You finally got the job you said you wanted, but instead of being happy you're perplexed because suddenly you feel like you're supposed to be doing something else with your life. You saved up all of your money to move to that city, but the housing deal didn't fall through.

Just when you thought you had your life all figured out, you start to see that none of your plans are working. So now what? Where do you go from here? How do you fix this? Why is this happening to you? Rest assured that your craving for success has turned into an appetite for God's will for your life. You're evolving. Your greatest accomplishments lie in your choice to let go of the familiar and walk in the unknown. It's okay not to know your next move. It's okay that none of your plans worked out. It's okay that you don't know what you're doing at this moment. When you humbly admit that you don't know what to do next, you create space for the unknown to manifest.

Knowing who you are both naturally and spiritually is more significant than knowing where you're going next. When you let God be your GPS the only thing you need to focus on is knowing how to drive your car. Just go! No matter how many times GPS reroutes; no matter how many delays are set out, as long as you know how to drive, GPS will get you to your destination from wherever you are currently located. You're not responsible for creating the directions... you're only responsible for following them. On your journey of elevation simply turn on your GPS, God's Perfect Strategy, and just drive!

PRAY WITH ME

Heavenly Father, thank you for being my GPS as I travel on this journey of elevation. As I continue to strive to fulfill my purpose on the earth, thank you for never steering me wrong. Thank you for every reroute, every detour, and every delay that I've already gone through or that I will encounter as I continue on this journey. Forgive me, Lord, for complaining when things didn't go the way I wanted them to go. I now understand that my thoughts are not your thoughts, and my ways are not your ways, but I am certain that you know best. Thank you for going ahead of me on my journey. Thank you for leading me and guiding me in the right direction. Condition my mind, Lord, to trust you fully. Condition my body, Lord, to walk by faith and not by sight. Condition my heart, Lord, to love like you, for out of my heart flows the issues of life. Condition my feet, Lord, to keep walking even when my body is telling me I'm too tired to go on. Relive me of the pressure that society has placed on me to fit their timeline of success. Lord, I trust you fully and give you total access to my past, present, and future. In Jesus' name, I pray, Amen.

READ WITH ME

Isaiah 30:21   Psalm 37:23-24   Proverbs 3: 5-6

John 14:26   Proverbs 20:18

CONNECT WITH ME

1. What are your plans for your life? Are you willing to change your plans if they are not in God's will for your life?

2. What things have you noticed about your original plans that no longer fit your current desires?

3. Who are you and who is your GPS?

4. What can you do to gain peace while you walk in the unknown of what's to come next?

REFLECTION

DAY 20:
LEVEL UP!
YOU'RE GOING PLACES

    I want to take this moment to give a major shoutout to a phenomenal young woman who's full of talent, faith, love, kindness, and beauty. So could you please give yourself a pat on the back because the woman I'm speaking of is you! Girl, you're all that plus more. I'm so proud of you. Now that you're in a place of walking in confidence, healing, positive vibes, favor, and the presence of God, it's time for you to level up. Leveling up means it's time for you to do some kingdom work. I know you thought this entire journey of elevation was all about you, but guess what? It's not.

    Your journey was strategically designed by God for you to be able to use your past pain, tests, trials, and testimonies to help someone else become free of their current situations so that they too can level up. It's time for you as a believer in Jesus Christ to ask what He is requiring of you. It's time that you ask God what your purpose in life is. It's time for you to be intentional about your daily activities. Everyone has a unique gift that can be used to glorify God. You may be saying to yourself, "I'm not an athlete, I'm not a singer, I'm not a hairstylist, nor am I a musician, so what's left for me to do?" Although those gifts are popular in society and extremely important, they are not the only important gifts and talents in the world.

    A clue God has given you about the purpose He has for your life is linked to the things you're naturally good at doing. For example, I'm naturally good at baking cakes, working with youth and millennials, teaching, and writing. What are you good at? Do you speak well in front of large crowds? Do you clean your house better than Mr. Clean himself? Can you write words, poems, or stories that will leave the toughest critics with tears in their eyes? Can you dance with great rhythm and grace? Can you cook a meal that makes a person's taste buds leap for joy? Are you extremely patient with others that need help? Do you work well with others in group settings? Are you good at math and enjoy working with numbers and finances? There is something special and unique about you that sets you apart from others around you. That very thing can be used to complete meaningful tasks on earth that glorify God.

    Don't be misled; you don't have to be a preacher or a deacon to do kingdom work. God wants you to be a light to someone else in the capacity that He has given you. Never minimize your gifts by comparing them to other people's gifts. If you weren't important or didn't have a purpose to fulfill then God would not have placed you on this earth. Don't be afraid to push beyond the borders of comfort and explore your gifts and talents. You may find that the very thing you're afraid of trying is something you're extremely good at doing.

    During meditation one morning, I began to hear the lyrics to a song playing in my head. So, I grabbed my phone, typed the name of the song on YouTube, and listened to the entire song several times. As I listened to the song, God told me I was going to perform a praise-dance routine to that song at my church the following Sunday. Before this moment, I had never performed a praise-dance routine in my life. I began to fuss with the Lord, explaining how I couldn't do it because I had never done it before. Guess who won the disagreement. That's right, the Lord. Later that day, God began to show me a vision of the routine to go along with the song that I had been listening to. After practicing the routine throughout the rest of the day, my body became undeniably tired.

    The next morning, I woke up to what felt like a ton of bricks laying on every muscle in my body. There were muscles that I didn't even know I had that ached with pain. I pushed through the pain and completed my daily duties.

When the time came for me to practice the routine again, I was so sore that I could barely pull off any of the original dance moves from the routine. I practiced it anyway! The next day held the same fate for my sore muscles and body. As I practiced the routine on the third day, the pain and soreness began to slowly fade away. While I was practicing, a girl who's a few years younger than me saw me dancing and asked if she could do the routine with me. I agreed and she quickly caught on to the steps of the routine. The following morning, we performed the routine together during church service. The experience was incredible.

    First and foremost, it was during meditation that I was pushed beyond my borders and comfort zone. It was in the time that I set aside for the Lord that I was able to hear from God regarding the new things he wanted me to do. Next, came obedience. I had to let go of my safe place and my comfort zone in order to tap into what the Lord instructed me to do. Obedience is better than sacrifice. Although the first day of practicing the routine was easy, the days after were hard-fought and challenging. I was new to praise dancing, so I had to condition my body to be able to handle the requirements of the routine. Anytime you level up and do something new, you will have to go through some sort of training and conditioning. The training and conditioning will cause you to stretch beyond your norm.

    Sometimes, it's not going to feel good to level up, but it's important to keep pushing through the pain because the pain you're experiencing now will benefit you and others later. Your success depends on your willingness to keep going after you start to feel the growing pains of elevation. In the beginning, the situation seemed to be all about me and my personal process of elevation, but soon after the final performance, God revealed to me the importance of me leveling up. When the young girl saw me practicing the praise-dance routine, it sparked her inner dancer and made her want to go beyond her borders and comfort zone also. Like me, she had never performed a praise-dance routine in front of an audience before our moment together. It didn't matter to her that I wasn't an expert or professional dancer. It only mattered that I was bold enough to do it in front of everyone at church. The Lord showed me how crucial it is to continue on my journey of elevation because someone else is waiting for me to level up so that they, too, can level up. If I would've been disobedient to God's instructions and not followed through with dance when he said to do so, I would've missed the divine opportunity to inspire someone else's growth. God didn't give me all the details in the beginning. He didn't tell me that I was going to be an example and inspiration to someone else. All he told me to do was dance.

In your season of leveling up, God is going to push you beyond the borders of your comfort zone. He is going to tell you to do things that make absolutely no sense at that moment. I encourage you to just do it. Just because God doesn't give you the blueprint, doesn't mean there isn't a plan. Trust in the Lord and the journey he has you on. In the end, you'll see that everything works out in your favor. Level up, mighty woman of God! Push through the barriers set before you. You're Going Places!

PRAY WITH ME

Father God, I thank you for every gift and every talent that you've placed down on the inside of me. I thank you for the visions, dreams, and goals that you've placed deep down in my heart. Lord, help me to understand who I am. Help me to understand my purpose on this earth. Help me to understand the gifts and talents that you've blessed me with. Build up my confidence so that I can operate at my full potential. Remove every spirit of doubt and insecurity that has hindered me from leveling up. Open my eyes so that I may see how special and important my unique gifts are. Give me a spirit of boldness so that I may walk into unknown places and own who I truly am. Strengthen me where I am weak and give me wisdom where I lack understanding. Forgive me for being slow to move. I now understand that someone is waiting on me to level up so that they too can level up. Teach me how to be an example. Teach me how to love myself and who I am unconditionally. Teach me how to use my gifts and talents to give your name glory. I humbly submit myself under your mighty hand. Speak to me so that I can hear your instructions clearly. I am a willing vessel for kingdom work. In Jesus' name, I pray, Amen.

READ WITH ME

Ephesians 2:10   2 Tim 1:7   Titus 2:7   1 Peter 4:10-11

CONNECT WITH ME

1. What are you good at?

2. Is there a career, job, or business that is related to the unique gifts/talents that you have?

3. How can you use your gifts/talents to help others and to give God glory?

4. What is stopping you from getting started?

REFLECTION

AUTHOR'S BIOGRAPHY

Chantoria Scott, also known as "Torre" by many friends and family members, is a 27-year-old visionary, influencer, and motivator. She established the brand "HER Elevation LLC" in 2018. HER Elevation LLC started as a teen mentor program, but then expanded as God gave Torre the vision to make the brand accessible to women of all ages. Chantoria also co-founded the internationally known group "The 4twelve Culture" in 2017. This group is devoted to using their gifts and talents to glorify God and being a positive influence for youth and adults.

Outside of her passion for writing, Torre's desire is to inspire, empower, and influence people through the love and knowledge of Christ Jesus. She is a minister in training, youth ambassador, teacher, leader, mentor, sister, aunt, author, writer, business owner, and inspirational/motivational speaker. In August of 2020, Torre released her first self-talk album, "Elevate" on all digital platforms. In December of

2020, Chantoria launched the podcast channel *Sublime Mindz*, available to listen to or stream on all podcast platforms. When she is not working in the school setting, Torre enjoys spending time with family and friends and participating in events with her church family at Victory Kingdom Worship Center in Greenville, SC.

Facebook @Her Elevation LLC
Instagram @her_elevation
Podcast Channel: Sublime Mindz

www.ingramcontent.com/pod-product-compliance
Lightning Source LLC
Chambersburg PA
CBHW032051150426
43194CB00006B/499